GREAT DOGS

of Albany and Beyond

EDITED BY PAUL GRONDAHL
AND TERESA BUCKLEY

TIMES UNION

A TIMES UNION PUBLICATION

GREAT DOGS
of Albany and Beyond

EDITED BY PAUL GRONDAHL
AND TERESA BUCKLEY

Portions of this book,
along with additional
photography
and videography,
are available at
http://timesunion.com/
greatdogs.
Join the conversation
by adding your stories to
the Web presentation.

TIMES UNION
P.O. Box 15000
645 Albany Shaker Road
Albany, New York 12212

ISBN 978-1-329-13886-5

TIMES UNION
A TIMES UNION PUBLICATION

Foreword

Brad Shear is executive director of the Mohawk Hudson Humane Society.

By Brad Shear

My family got our first dog when I was 8 years old. He was a little Yorkie named Fang who was born at the neighbor's house. His name came from a New Yorker cartoon, though it may just as well have come from the fact that he had a tendency to bite the ankles of visitors. In addition to biting, he was never house trained and we came home to a fresh accident every day for 18 years.

We lived on the fourth floor of an apartment building in New York City and my father would take him for walks in the rain, on the coldest nights and hottest weather. My mother would cook ground beef and gizzards for him while my brother and I might be sent to the corner for a slice of pizza. And we loved that little dog.

Why did we tolerate so much from this fluffy little 10-pound creature? Maybe because of the excitement he couldn't contain every time we came home, or the big eyes he would stare at us with when he was hungry, or the way he would rub his head against our hands when he wanted attention.

We receive unconditional love from our dogs and that above all is what connects us. They offer companionship without judgment or reserve.

Dogs and people evolved together over thousands of years. That coevolution has intertwined our species in a way that is unique in the animal kingdom. Recent studies suggest that when we look into our dogs' eyes our bodies release oxytocin, a hormone that is associated with social bonding, making us feel good and reducing anxiety. Those of us with dogs don't need to be told we feel good when we're with our dogs, looking in their eyes, petting them or playing a good game of fetch.

The relationship between us and our dogs is evolving. At one time, most dogs had a job such as herding, protecting or hunting. At the same time, when not working, those dogs often were the family pet. It was only the elite who had the resources to have a dog who was strictly a companion. Those dogs were small, meant to be attractive accessories and symbols of status.

As we became more urban, most dogs became companions and most of us are able to have our own companions with no other expectation than to love and be loved by them. We have birthday parties for our dogs, take them on vacation and sleep with them.

In February 1996, my perspective on our relationship with dogs changed forever when I arrived on my first day at the Humane Society of Boulder Valley. I had been hired to take care of animals in the kennels and people at the front desk. What I did not expect was, when you tell someone you work at the Humane Society, they like to tell you stories about their dogs.

Nineteen years later, I have heard countless stories about dogs who enriched the lives of their families. With the advent of smartphones, I usually get to see a photo and sometimes a video. I discovered that every dog has a story. The stories are unique to each dog and family, but in a way they are all the same. They are all stories of the connections people have made with their best friends, the stories of constant companions who touched people and will be remembered as an essential member of the family.

I feel blessed and honored that people share with me their stories of the special relationship they have with their dogs. Now, in this book, they will share them with you.

3

A word from
our donors

The Times Union is grateful to the donors who, by underwriting this book's production, are helping to support the Mohawk Hudson Humane Society and the Times Union Hope Fund.

Some people have asked us why we support the work of the Humane Society and animal rescue. We are, in fact, dog lovers. Dogs are not our whole life, but they make our lives whole. And we know that a dog is the only thing on earth that loves you more than he loves himself.

Of course, the world would be a nicer place if everyone had the ability to love as unconditionally as a dog. Once you have a wonderful dog, life without one is a life diminished.

The people whose stories are in this book would surely agree with us that sometimes when you think you need a helping hand and you reach out, what you get is, thankfully, a loving paw.

— Chet and Karen Opalka

In addition to **Chet and Karen Opalka,** these generous donors contributed to the "Great Dogs of Albany and Beyond" book project:

Tony Bifaro

Alan Goldberg

Goldstein Auto Group

E. Stewart Jones Hacker Murphy Law Firm

Kinderhook Bank

Kathleen McNamee

Morris & McVeigh Law Firm

Mr. and Mrs. Ronald Riggi

Contents

Contents

How the Great Dogs book project began

By Paul Grondahl

Paul Grondahl has been a Times Union staff writer since 1984, has written several books and is a lifelong dog lover.

For several days after the column appeared, emails, phone calls, letters and sympathy cards arrived at the newspaper – more than 300. They were heartfelt, personal and touching messages of sympathy. Some of the letters ran several pages and included photographs.

I have written more than 7,000 articles for the Times Union over the past 30 years, some 6 million words, and nothing in my experience had drawn that kind of response from readers.

There had been a death in the family and I wrote a story about it. We had made the difficult decision to let go of our beloved Daisy, a 14-year-old black Labrador retriever, and we asked our veterinarian to release her from chronic pain and debilitating old age.

Each letter began with kind expressions of sympathy, but they did not stop there. The column had sparked a conversation. The writers took the time to tell me about a great dog they had loved and how much that dog had meant to their lives. My column had struck a chord and elicited something meaningful and truly deep inside each of them: the unconditional love, unfailing companionship and unwavering loyalty a dog had given them.

One reader wrote that her father with Alzheimer's disease cannot remember the names of any of his children or grandchildren; the only name he can remember is the dog's. Others described the work of their therapy dogs who assist children with autism or residents of nursing homes or youths with emotional disabilities. Many wrote about rescuing dogs and someone sent a photo of a bumper sticker that summed up the themes of those stories: "Who Rescued Whom?"

I read and responded to all these lovely communications. I saved them all in a thick file folder on a shelf next to my desk. I told my editors they were so powerful and authentic that they could form the foundation of a good book one day. They liked the idea. But more stories, other assignments and the urgency of relentless deadlines buried the dog stories in a stack of paper and notebooks.

More than a year passed.

I came to think of the people who wrote to me as Dog People. I count myself among them. There are far more Dog People than I imagined. In the four-county Capital Region, nearly 125,000 of the 342,135 households own a dog or more than one, bringing the estimated total to 212,000.

And each and every single one of those owners thinks their dog is the greatest, the best dog ever.

Love is blind in matters of the heart, including a person's love of a dog. It cuts both ways. Dogs are social animals that derive equal amounts of pleasure from the bond they share with their two-legged companions.

The human-canine bond reaches back thousands of years to when dogs were first domesticated. There's more than a grain of truth in the cliche "man's best friend," first coined a few

"I came to think of the people who wrote to me as Dog People. I count myself among them. And each and every single one of those owners thinks their dog is the greatest, the best dog ever."

centuries ago. The connection between dogs and their human owners has been probed by anthropologists, psychologists and sociologists. It gave rise to the notion of anthropomorphism: attributing human characteristics and behavior to dogs.

The American Veterinary Medical Association confirmed that a powerful human-canine bond has existed from time immemorial and that the physical, emotional and psychological interactions between the two promote well-being in both.

The dozens of contributors to this book are quintessential Dog People.

They wrote stories of rescue dogs with grim histories who were reclaimed and rehabilitated by a family's love. They shared hilarious anecdotes about a dog who barked if its owner forgot its order of small fries at the McDonald's drive-through; a pooch who slurped champagne from a crystal flute; a single-minded dog who consistently filched its owner's lacy undergarments.

One wrote a story of family dogs divided between homes after a divorce, and of exes who came back together for the first time in several years in a tender moment of reunion to mourn the passing of a sweet dog whose love they once shared. It was a touching example of the extraordinary healing powers of dogs.

One man wrote that he hated to admit it, but he grieved more for a wonderful dog of his than he did for some of his relatives who had passed away.

It is telling that when you read the obituaries in the Times Union each morning, as I do, that several of the lives summarized in 600 words or so include the name of a beloved dog.

This book is a celebration of all the ways that great dogs enrich our lives.

Reader-submitted stories form the heart of this book. They complement stories written by Times Union staff members and me on our family dogs, including our new dog, Lily; Albany's famous historical dogs Nipper and Owney; governors' dogs who lived at the Executive Mansion and more.

Proceeds from "Great Dogs of Albany and Beyond" will benefit the Mohawk Hudson Humane Society and the Times Union Hope Fund, which sends disadvantaged youths to summer camps and after-school programs.

For the Dog People whose stories are included in this book and for those who do not yet know they are Dog People, we invite you to enjoy these stories about how our lives are immeasurably enriched by great dogs.

It has been suggested that all dogs go to heaven and that dog is god spelled backward. You won't hear an argument from us.

Paul Grondahl
May 5, 2015

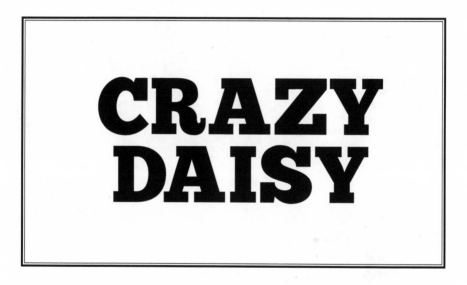

Saying goodbye to Daisy, a great family dog

By Paul Grondahl

I lifted Daisy, our 14-year-old black Lab, from the back seat of the car. I placed her gently onto a brown blanket spread on the floor of the veterinarian's exam room. Caroline stroked Daisy's gray muzzle, which rested in her lap. It was a week after Caroline's 18th birthday, two weeks after her high school graduation and less than two months before she left for college.

Now, another passage awaited, one we had dreaded for months. Daisy became incontinent, and her hind legs began to wobble and teeter like an old broken gate. With each fresh indignity, more of the spark went out of her brown eyes.

Last week, those deep pools of soulfulness seemed to beseech us to let her go with dignity. She was 98 in dog years and we had crossed a fine line between a desire to keep Daisy in our lives and to do what was humane for the dog.

My wife, Mary, sat on a bench in the room and clutched Daisy's collar. I stretched out on the floor and spoke to Daisy in a soothing voice and told her over and over what a great dog she was. I rubbed her ears and the velvety tips still felt puppy-soft. There was a box of tissues and we each began to empty its contents.

We had given the puppy to Caroline as a surprise

Photos courtesy of Caroline Grondahl

Caroline and Daisy, best companions for 14 years.

gift on her fourth birthday. Caroline's face radiated pure joy as a small black fuzzy ball of mischief scuffled behind her and licked her arm. I captured that moment in a photograph.

She named her Daisy. This was several months after we put down Jazz, our black Lab mix, at 13. Few things can compare with a childhood shaped by the unconditional love of a dog. We wanted that bond for Caroline. Daisy was the first purebred I had ever bought after adopting dogs from the pound. We got her from a breeder who worked with my wife.

I took Caroline to play with the puppies on a pretext a few weeks before her birthday, and she gravitated to Daisy,

the runt of the litter.

I think she felt sorry for the timid little pup who got pushed around by her more aggressive siblings.

Daisy came with an AKC certificate and a folder that included a family tree detailing her championship pedigree. I lost the paperwork, but the breeder had leveled with me. Daisy could never be a show dog because she had small white patches behind her front paws and other slight imperfections. She was a family pet who was never a champion in anything except this: the love she brought into our lives was world-class.

She deserved some kind of ribbon for her appetite. She was never finicky and ate the same brand of dry dog food her entire life. When she heard the nuggets hit her stainless steel bowl, she began to perform what we called "the dinner dance." It was a spinning, whirling dervish motion in which all four paws lost contact with the ground. She could Hoover a cup's worth in less than 30 seconds. Even in her final days, she did the dinner dance, a slow and creaky version with a single rotation, before plowing into her food. She never left anything in the bowl.

I left her in the garage once after we moved into our new house when Daisy was 3 years old and she chewed off long strips of drywall tape and joint compound. She never destroyed shoes we left around the house, except for the plastic tips of the shoe-laces in my running sneakers. I caught her crunching those a few times like so many ca-shews. If I tried to scold her, she would scamper around the house in a move we called "the butt scooch." It resem-bled a Roadrunner cartoon and spawned her nickname: Crazy Daisy.

Labs are known to love the water and their webbed feet make them strong swimmers. Not Daisy. She was a wader who preferred to galumph in the shallows as she chewed clumps of pond grass. We tried several times to carry Daisy out into deep water and to coax her into swimming in ponds, lakes, rivers and the ocean. No go.

She also had an aversion to stairs. She lived her entire

Daisy at rest in our backyard, her favorite spot.

life on the ground floor of our house. We tried many induce-ments, but none worked. She slept on a blanket on a love seat in the TV room and was content. Once we rented a motel room in Provincetown on Cape Cod for a long week-end because it allowed dogs. I did not realize the room was on the second floor until we arrived and the only ac-cess was an outdoor wooden stairway. I tried everything, but Daisy would not budge. I ended up carrying her 70 pounds — four legs locked at full extension —up and down the stairs three times a day. She was usually sandy and wet from the beach. The guests gave us a wide berth.

An obedience class early on had little effect and our attempts at training became sporadic and half-hearted.

Daisy was a jumper and a flopper. She jumped up onto anyone who came to our house in an exuberant greeting. I could not break her of the habit until arthritis did at age 10. On walks, when

we passed another dog, she immediately flopped onto her back in a submissive posture. She did not possess an ag-gressive bone in her body. She even flopped for cats. Daisy loved all creatures great and small.

Daisy had champion traits. She was a pro at curling up at my feet as I wrote in my study, immovable for hours at a time. No dog was better to watch movies with because she never stirred.

Each morning as I came downstairs, Daisy greeted me with a full-body wag. I reciprocated with a bear hug. She groaned with pleasure. She brought out good traits in us, like love and tolerance and gentleness. I thought of a magnet my parents have on their refrigerator: "I aspire to be the person my dog thinks I am." We felt that way about Daisy.

In the vet's office, the drugs did their work. Daisy slipped away, silently and peacefully. Time seemed to stand still. We had been there for an hour, saying our long goodbyes. The tissue box was empty. I looked back one last time at the black mound on the brown blanket on the floor. We closed the door quietly behind us and carried out into the lengthen-ing shadows the memory of a great dog, our beloved Daisy, a true champion in the things that mattered.

▶ *This article first appeared in the Times Union in July 2013.*

The global reach of The Rainbow Bridge

By Paul Grondahl

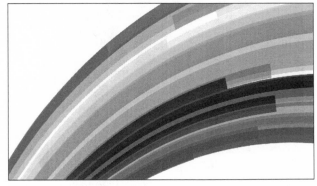

Among the hundreds of condolence cards, emails and calls I received after I wrote a column about the death of our beloved dog, Daisy, several referred to the Rainbow Bridge.

These readers intended it as a comfort and suggested that Daisy had gone to a better place and that the two of us would be reunited, over the Rainbow Bridge one day.

I had never heard of the Rainbow Bridge and didn't know what these well-meaning people meant until a couple of thoughtful readers added a copy of the poem.

It is more prose than verse and it is highly stylized and sentimental. Still, it possesses an undeniable pull and has gained extraordinary reach and legions of fans around the world. It is best read by someone who has recently lost a pet with a box of tissues close at hand.

Although its provenance is officially listed as "author unknown," the poem has been widely distributed on the Internet for more than a decade and was believed to have been written sometime in the 1980s.

There have been more than a dozen books, aimed at children and adults, that incorporate the Rainbow Bridge poem as a way of helping cope with the loss of a beloved pet.

At least three authors have been suggested as the creator of "The Rainbow Bridge," but no one has come forward formally to claim credit.

The poem bears elements of Norse mythology and is based on a long-held notion of a paradise where pets are happily reunited with their owners.

The poem is not copyrighted and is widely republished and reproduced.

"The Rainbow Bridge"

There is a bridge connecting Heaven and Earth. It is called the Rainbow Bridge because of its many colors. Just this side of the Rainbow Bridge there is a land of meadows, hills and valleys with lush green grass.

When a beloved pet dies, the pet goes to this place. There is always food and water and warm spring weather. All the animals who have been ill and old are restored to health and vigor; those who were hurt or maimed are made whole and strong again, just as we remember them in our dreams of days and times gone by.

The animals are happy and content, except for one small thing; they each miss someone very special to them, who had to be left behind. They all run and play together, but the day comes when one suddenly stops and looks into the distance. Her bright eyes are intent; her eager body begins to quiver. Suddenly she begins to run from the group, flying over the green grass, her legs carrying her faster and faster. You have been spotted, and when you and your special friend finally meet, you cling together in joyous reunion. The happy kisses rain upon your face; your hands again caress the beloved head, and you look once more into the trusting eyes of your pet, so long gone from your life but never absent from your heart.

Then you cross the Rainbow Bridge together, never again to be separated.

— Poem's author unknown

Quest for food never stopped Kosmo

By Dianne L. Patterson

Our sheltie Kosmo was named after Cosmo Kramer of the "Seinfeld" TV show because he was always looking for an angle. The focus of his angling was food, food and food. That's not unusual for a dog, of course, but Kosmo employed strategy — technique, even, in his quests.

Bringing in groceries from the car one day, I foolishly put them briefly on the floor. After putting everything away, I was eager to make lunch. Where was the pound of turkey? In the car? Still at the store? The bigger question was, "Where was Kosmo?" In the basement, I found him behind the couch finishing the turkey. He knew to hide — an entire floor away — to give himself enough time to eat before I missed him.

Once, when he was just a puppy, a bag of bread went missing from the counter. I looked high and low. How do you lose a loaf of bread? I later found it — half of it, rather — in his crate. The last place I looked should have been the first place I looked.

At a sitter's house, he broke through a fortress of gates and bungee cords to reach large Tupperware containers of dog food. The sitter said no other dog had done that — not the claim to fame we wanted. He wasn't invited back.

While we hosted a dinner during Kosmo's later years, guests yelled for my attention. Kosmo's food-gathering technique had taken on that of a magician. He was backing away from the table with the tablecloth in his mouth, dragging casseroles, meats and gravies in his direction.

He used the same technique on our Christmas tree at just 6 months old. With a strand of lights in his mouth, he pulled until the tree came down. I think he was after the candy canes.

While sometimes entertaining, his antics grew increasingly frustrating. "Who forgot to put the garbage away

Photos courtesy of Dianne L. Patterson
Painting of Kosmo the sheltie and Kosmo begging for food.

before leaving?" was a common question in our house, immediately followed by, "Come down here and clean up Kosmo's mess!"

He even put himself in the hospital with his overindulgences — once with pancreatitis and once with kidney failure. Other times, the diagnoses were not so life-threatening, and the hospital stays not so long or expensive. Even with all his shenanigans, he was still tops in my book. In fact, not long after Kosmo passed, my son and I were watching a television show focused on the parents' favorite child. My son, an only child, thought he'd be cute by asking me if he was my favorite. You should have seen the look on his face when I said, "Now that Kos is gone you are!"

▶ *Contributor Dianne L. Patterson lives in Albany.*

The lucky number turned up Rudy the poster pup

By Gina Giuliano

I was uncertain I'd get another dog right away after 15-year-old Howie died. I read a Times Union story about Sandy, a beagle, and her puppies, born September 1995 at Mohawk Hudson Humane Society. They also appeared on Steve Caporizzo's Pet Connection on TV.

I called the shelter daily about adopting. When I eventually visited and saw the crowd waiting, I was both optimistic and melancholy. The attendants drew numbers, with each person called able to choose a "poster" puppy. I wanted a puppy, but I didn't want to choose!

One puppy remained when my number, 29, magically was drawn. The attendant handed me a tri-colored fluff.

I named him "Rudy," after New York City's mayor, whose surname is one letter different from mine.

Handsome on the inside and out, Rudy was the happiest dog ever, always wagging his tail, never pensive. He was immaculate in appearance, hating when his white fur was dirty. He was mischievous, holding things (underwear, coins, paper) hostage until he received ransom — a treat.

As a puppy, he chewed up shoes, furniture, books and my husband's thesis. He destroyed window screens, too.

Although quite a handful as a youngster, he was a mellow adult. He loved all people, even those who didn't care for dogs. He liked to sniff human

Photo courtesy of Gina Giuliano

Rudy the beagle with a Stewart's milk carton.

ears and hair, and from his perch on the stairs would persist until visitors let him.

Despite hound ancestry, he didn't hunt, but he spent hours by the window, keeping watch over the village.

He especially loved winter. His favorite activity was rolling in snow; I remember feeling joy watching him wiggle on his back after a storm. I called him "arctic dog" when he came inside, his body coated with snow.

He loved "dens" — private areas to curl up. He created one under the daybed that remained a lifelong favorite place. Another was under a shrub in the yard; we still refer to this as Rudy's bush.

I didn't train him — no crates, no obedience. Rudy taught himself to be well-be-

haved. I did teach him tricks: "paw," "speak" and "sit."

One day in January 2005, there was blood in the snow. Multiple vet visits followed. Rudy died a week after his 10th birthday. He had no old-age warts, no gray fur, no declining senses. His coat was shiny and there was no sign of tartar on his teeth. He still howled at the mailman, played with toys and never failed to greet us. It was eventually apparent that cancer was causing weight loss.

Ten years was too short to have this wonderful dog. The luckiest day of my life was when my number was drawn and I got to take home the last of the "poster pups."

▶ *Contributor Gina Giuliano lives in Castleton.*

Caesar brought love and joy to a lively household

By Brittany Horn

Photo courtesy of Brittany Horn

Caesar, the golden retriever, with Brittany Horn.

I don't quite trust people who don't like dogs. Then again, maybe I'm biased.

I fell in love at the age of 9 with a short, chubby golden retriever puppy staring into my eyes. He was warm, fluffy and everything that I'm sure my mom didn't want wreaking havoc on her house. But Dad had promised.

Things became a lot hairier and without realizing it, my family's hearts began to grow. Caesar was a dog for the books and he made our lives richer.

One afternoon, Caesar walked to my grandfather's auto shop a block away from our home, leaving my mom and me hoarse from yelling his name in the backyard. Then the house phone rang.

"You'll never believe who just showed up," my grandfather said. "Caesar just crossed the street and came right on in the front door."

We never figured out how he pulled it off. In the end, the story is probably better without us knowing.

Dogs come into our lives to help us learn about the world and the people in it, especially ourselves. They teach us humility and how to hide a drool stain; forgiveness and how to deliver the best big kiss; but most of all, they teach us love in its purest, most unconditional form.

And Caesar was no different — the best secret-keeper I knew and an ever better big spoon. If I spend most of my later years passed out on a big sofa with the people I love, I'll consider it a good life.

That's exactly how Caesar spent the last few years of his life, spoiled rotten and often covered up with one of our childhood comforters, moving only with the aid of his best friend and caretaker — my mom — and the promise of a long car ride or a peanut butter bone. Though Caesar was my birthday gift, my mom was the first love on his list (and in just this one case, I'll happily take second place).

In Caesar's last summer with us, I was gifted with my last few months off before starting my big-girl job in the fall and moving out of the house for good. The two of us spent most of our afternoons together. Every so often, we would load up into the car for a trip to the vet or a car ride.

Occasionally, we'd move a little slower. I'd sit down in the grass as Caesar let out a loud "harumph" to let me know he wasn't a fan.

"Getting old's a bitch," I could hear him say in the same voice I hear from my grandpa. And I'd cradle his face, kiss him on the nose, and tell him I know.

No one warned me how to say goodbye. Our childhood dogs seem like they'll live forever. But then comes the day when they don't.

Far and away, Caesar was the best thing to ever happen to my family. He brought joy, laughter and more barking to my crazy house than I would have ever dreamed. And every day, we miss him.

So until I see him again, I will imagine him, his nose turned skyward, waiting for the next peanut butter bone and sectional sofa.

▶ *Brittany Horn is a former Hearst fellow and Times Union reporter.*

Sunny's greatest escape

By Michael Huber

What makes my golden mix the best dog ever? Let me take you back to his earlier days. Come with Sunny and me as we relive his greatest escape.

Sunny is, technically, what's known as a golden-doodle, but that pretentious portmanteau seems unfitting for an animal that does his business outside and licks himself silly in a manner that makes me blush.

First, you need to understand Sunny is a runner. If Sunny sees an opening, a door the tiniest bit ajar or a gate closed with an imperfect latch, he'll make a break for it. Gotta respect a dog that tests his boundaries.

Whenever Sunny escaped and subsequently was captured after ambling around the neighborhood, returning in shame with his head hung low, his little doggy brain started plotting his next getaway, I'm sure of it. From his perch on the couch, he'd sit and ponder his next escape, like Steve McQueen in "Papillon."

The school bus.

Sunny picked up the routine. Mondays through Fridays, like clockwork, he'd hear the school bus turn the corner, watch it slow to a stop in front of the house and see Julia and Jack clamber up the little stairway to freedom.

Sure, the kids returned each afternoon, but since this was elementary school, the kids hopped happily off that bus. Wherever they had gone,

Photo courtesy of Michael Huber

Jack and Julia and Sunny Huber at their home in Delmar.

Sunny wanted a piece of it.

It was a crisp, early fall day. I'm not sure what happened that morning, but the school bus arrived before we got to the curb. I also don't remember who opened the front door, but I do remember who was the first one through.

Boom. Swoosh. A blur bolted past my legs, like a shooting star of doggy fur. Sunny galloped down the driveway. He could have made a run for the hills, but instead, he bounded up the school bus stairs like a soldier going home on leave.

The kids on the bus squealed! I ran to the bus, in terror that my pup might take a chunk out of a kid's leg. Percy the Bus Driver, a big bear of a man who loved his job, laughed and laughed. "It's fine, it's fine," he bellowed in

his Louis Armstrong voice.

As I turned down the aisle to escort Sunny off the bus, I saw the kids' faces. I have never seen children as happy as I did that day. A fluffy dog on the bus going to school? No way! This is the Best Day Ever!

Those kids are in high school now. Sunny is a middle-aged dog. Me too, I suppose. He walks a bit slower and doesn't have the pluck of his younger years. Me too. I wonder, when I see him on the couch looking out the window, does he watch the school bus pass by each morning and think back to the time he was filled with elementary school energy?

▶ *Contributor Michael Huber lives in Delmar and works at the Times Union.*

Guinness loved family, car rides and food

By Maryann Kelly

Photo courtesy of Maryann Kelly

Guinness, a chocolate Labrador retriever.

Guinness came into our life at a bittersweet time — we had just celebrated the birth of a great-niece and shortly after that the death of our sister Patty.

Guinness was a beautiful chocolate Lab who loved three things in life: his human family (my brother Bill Kelly and me), car rides and food.

Once, when we had gone grocery shopping and stocked the fridge with our favorite foods, my brother and I decided to run some errands.

When we returned, Guinness was lying in front of an open refrigerator door with several empty plastic deli bags around him and he was about to eat a big juicy steak.

He saw us standing there and I swear he had a smile on his face. When I realized what he had already eaten, I don't think it was a smile, but more like heartburn. It didn't take us long to see what he had gotten into — a pound of turkey, a pound of roast beef and a pound of cheese. To this day, I do not know how he got the fridge door open.

Guinness was also known to eat entire loaves of bread, including the wrapper, and to eat a piece of pizza from a closed box without anyone knowing about it. I always said he had a stomach of steel. After those incidents, we called him, "dough boy" and "bread basket."

Guinness loved going on car rides. He didn't care how long or short the rides were, just as long as he was with one or both of us. He would sit in the front seat and look out the window just watching the world go by. When one of us got out of the car, Guinness' eyes never left the door that we entered. As soon as he saw us come out of the door, his tail would start to thump and he would get so excited his whole body would shake.

We took him everywhere with us, but I think his favorite place to visit was Cape Cod. He loved to run on the beach and chase the waves. He wouldn't go far without looking back to make sure we were there watching him.

Even when I came home and found garbage all over the house and he got yelled at, he knew we loved him. He would sit next to me on the couch with his head on my lap and look up at me with those big soulful eyes and I knew exactly what he was thinking. I would bend over and whisper in his ear, "I love you too, Guin."

When Guinness became sick, we knew our time with him was soon going to end. One day, my great-niece, Erin, who was about 8 at the time, was at our house watching her mom brush him, his fur flying in all different directions. She asked me if I had a little box. I told her where she could find one. With the box in her hand, she started to pick up pieces of his fur and put them inside. As she was leaving, she handed me the box and on it she had written, "Now you will always have a piece of Guinness with you."

I will never part with that box; it will be with me forever.

Guinness passed away on March 16, 2009, at the age of 14. Rest in peace, my precious Guinness. I hope you are enjoying a great feast in heaven.

▶ *Contributor Maryann Kelly lives in Clifton Park.*

Maggie chews up everything in her path

By Donna Liquori

First, Maggie ate the top of the upholstered heirloom footstool that was one of my late mother-in-law's cherished possessions.

Then she ripped a hole in the leather cushion of the ancient club chair that my husband sat in when he got in trouble as a teen. He sat there a lot so you'd think he'd have more patience for our puppy's wayward behavior.

Then she destroyed the "Christmas Story" leg lamp wire cord, which was, thankfully, not plugged in. Maggie seems to zero in on the things my husband treasures, which is funny considering he's the one who didn't want a dog.

Other things that have found their way into Maggie's mouth: ancient nails that she clawed up from between floor boards in our old house, the insole of an L.L. Bean boot, a Mac Air power cord, two sets of headphones, wayward bagels, molding. Luckily, she didn't swallow anything bad before I got to her and now our house is dog-proofed.

She's the first dog we've had as a family and, despite her mischief, we're all pretty much head over heels — even my husband.

Maggie's got her own space — her crate and the laundry room — but she's become a constant companion. She sleeps with us when I give in to her cries. She curls up on the couch during movie night and hangs out in the yard on a tether while we garden.

Maggie is what we used to call a mutt. Now, we make up names for mixed breed dogs. She is a "schnuggle," a combination of schnauzer, pug and beagle. From different angles, she captures each one of those breeds. Her fur or hair seems to be all schnauzer and even though I'm allergic to dogs, I've experienced no reactions.

She stands a foot high at the present time, except she tried to eat the measuring tape so I'm not quite sure. We think at 9 months, she's fully grown. She weighs maybe 12 pounds.

Despite her small stature, she holds her own at the dog park — a tiny black blur whipping around the legs of the bigger dogs, sometimes stealing their balls and generally being a pest. It's hysterical.

Maggie was technically a rescue dog. Her mother was brought in while pregnant with pups that were born here in a safe place. We had most of them at our house to make our choice. They clambered over us and ran around like crazy, tackling each other and us in the process. My youngest daughter got her wish for Maggie and we agreed.

Magnolia is her full name, for the two front yard magnolia trees given to me for our first Mother's Days in this house almost two decades ago.

There was some confusion at first; "male" was written on the adoption papers and when we investigated physically, I couldn't really figure it out. So we renamed her Louie for a bit until taking her back to the rescue place for verification.

For the moment, the club chair is safe. The vintage footstool has been removed from the parlor and I've started looking for upholsterers. As for the leg lamp, well, I suppose it will need to be rewired. As Maggie trains us in our new role as a dog family, the adjustments we've had to make are all about love.

▶ *Contributor Donna Liquori lives in Delmar and is a regular Times Union contributor.*

Photo courtesy of Donna Liquori

Maggie loves to chew on whatever she can find.

Minnie arrived, and rearranged the furniture

By Claire Lynch

It was Christmas week 1999 and the holidays were in full swing. In the midst of the hustle and bustle of the season, I sat down to watch the TV news, and Steve Caporizzo was reading his Christmas poem for homeless animals.

He showed photos of animals at the Mohawk Hudson Humane Society. I spotted a dog that looked like the dog we had when I was young — a purebred long-haired German shepherd we named Dudley.

Dudley was a great dog. I needed to see if this dog was anything like Dudley.

The next morning, I was at the shelter. I knew I had to have her.

I named her Minnie. She came home with me on Dec. 26, 1999. The vet at the shelter thought Minnie was about 1.

I had taken time off from work so I could get Minnie used to her new home. She seemed to adjust well, and I enjoyed having the company.

I planned to keep Minnie in the kitchen while I was at work. I left her behind the gate with her food, water and toys.

When I returned home, I opened the front door and thought for certain I had been robbed. The hallway was strewn with garbage and the living room furniture was moved all around. The gate was up with no dog in sight. When I called Minnie, her head popped up from the sofa.

I surveyed the damage. This crazy dog had taken hold

Photo courtesy of Claire Lynch

Minnie, the shepherd mix, on the dog bed she hated.

of the skirting on the sofa and loveseat and pulled the furniture around with her teeth.

Minnie looked at me as if to say, "I did OK today, didn't I?"

She loved McDonald's fries. Our routine when we went for a ride was to pull into the drive-through and get her a small order of fries. If I didn't stop, she would bark to remind me.

She was curious, sometimes to a fault. She was skunked once and we never did that again.

Each spring, during our walks along the river, we would see a pair of ducks named Gertrude and Heathcliff, soon to hatch some ducklings. Minnie watched them as they walked about but never bothered them.

We had our down times. Minnie had separation anxiety. She developed colitis and started having seizures. We became regulars at Parkside

Veterinary Hospital.

We had had 10 years together when she started to go downhill. I would have done anything to keep Minnie with me, but I had to make the decision that it was time to say goodbye to my friend. When she was gone, I got in my car and cried until I didn't think tears would come.

A few days later, the vet called to say that they had Minnie's collar and tags. That day was almost harder than the goodbye. All I had left was that red collar. Those tags have been on my key ring since that day.

In my prayers, I asked God for a sign that Minnie was OK and happy. The answer came as I walked out the door. Sitting on my patio were Gertrude and Heathcliff.

It was the sign I needed.

▶ *Contributor Claire Lynch lives in Albany.*

Spike, the thief of clothing and hearts

By Kimberly Matthews

Spike was a thief. From the night we first brought him home, he started stealing things. And, like any other thief, he was not inclined to give things back.

His favorite thing to steal was a towel, either from the kitchen or the bathroom, depending on which one was more accessible at the time.

Spike was a large dog — a mix of chocolate Lab, Rottweiler and French mastiff — so there wasn't much he couldn't reach.

Occasionally he would slow down to an arrogant trot, with his head and tail held high. He loved nothing more than grabbing the kitchen towel off of the oven door and racing off with it. He would stare directly at me, taunting me with it. But the second I attempted to retrieve it, he would dart off again with a gleeful growl.

In his youth, especially, he was not shy about tearing the towel apart in front our faces.

If we tried to discipline him with a newspaper, he would steal that, too.

Spike would pretty much steal anything, so long as it brought him attention. He stole cookies off the kitchen counter; he regularly dug out my underwear from the laundry bin; he stole presents from under the Christmas tree; he stole socks — oftentimes right off our feet; he stole stuffed animals.

Countless times, I got out of the shower only to realize

Photo courtesy of Jim Matthews

Spike, a mix of chocolate Lab, Rottweiler and French mastiff, in the snow with Kimberly Matthews.

that some article of clothing had gone missing. There was no such thing as "fetch" with Spike. He was like a broken boomerang.

If by some chance Spike was not interested in stealing a particular thing, he made sure no one else wanted it, either. He achieved this by wiping his sloppy jowls on whatever that thing might be. This was especially true of new clothing.

Spike stole the show everywhere he went. When we took him out for walks, people stopped to pet him and comment on how beautiful his markings were.

When we took him to Julian, Calif., in the winter, he would pounce and prance in the snow, ensuring that all eyes were on him.

When we took him to the beach, he would chase birds and bark like a puppy.

If we were ever to have extended conversations with friends, Spike would begin to

growl and grunt, eager to get in on the conversation. There was no upstaging him.

Spike was most guilty of stealing our hearts, but his own heart was the one thing that he did not hesitate to share with us.

Spike was also a guardian. He was steadfast in his role as household protector. ADT ain't got nothing on Spike. He provided a true sense of safety. In public, he kept a large radius around us, ensuring that no other dog shared in our affections. If any other dog came to greet us, Spike would chase it out like a jealous lover.

His mischievous antics will forever be on our minds and we will never forget his unique personality. Such a boring thing to now have all of our items where we left them.

▶ *Contributed by Kimberly Matthews via longtime Capital Region resident Jim Matthews, who lives in California.*

Chasing Buckley the hound on Christmas

By Jennifer E. O'Brien

Dignified. Sweet natured. Friendly. None of these adjectives describe Buckley, our beagle basset mix that we affectionately dubbed our "bastard hound." But after driving more than three hours north to Saranac Lake to adopt him, he was family.

Just like any family member, he filled us with joy and angst, occasionally at the same time.

Our first Christmas together as a family with Buckley was in 2003. We had hosted Christmas Eve and made the big announcement to our families that we were expecting our first child in August 2004. Christmas morning was spent putting the house back in order and that meant taking Buckley's crate from the garage and putting it back in the house.

As Lew and I navigated the crate back in the front door, he slipped out and took off. This was his fourth time getting out in as many months.

Because our house sat at the end of a cul-de-sac and was adjacent to woods, getting him back was always a challenge.

We took off in our pajamas, chasing him down the street. The faster we ran, the more he dug in for a good race.

In and out of unknown neighbors' backyards, we shouted his name and, in desperation started flinging

Photos courtesy of Jennifer E. O'Brien

Buckley, a beagle basset mix.

full-size hot dogs in his direction. What a sight we were for unsuspecting families just waking to open their presents. Winded and unsuccessful, we went back for the car and started on his trail again.

We spotted him again and jumped out of the car, hoping to nab him. He was smiling broadly and still bounding joyfully away from us. This was the greatest game of chase ever.

It was a white Christmas that year, and so, in a last-ditch effort, Lew tackled him in a snowbank. Finally, we got him.

Once Lew got the leash back on Buckley and caught his breath, they started walking back home. The whole time, Buckley's smile

Buckley with O'Brien's daughter, Caroline Dubuque.

never wavered and his tail kept a-waggin'. Merry Christmas indeed!

▶ *Contributor Jennifer E. O'Brien lives in East Greenbush.*

Max the jumbo sheltie and his odd diet

Max, a jumbo-sized Shetland sheepdog.

By Norma Chepaitis Shook

We got Max in 2007, six months after losing our beloved blue merle sheltie, Bonnie.

We had a 10-year-old rescue sheltie, Mickey, and we all needed happiness again, so in our 50s, in a moment or two of insanity, we brought home a sheltie puppy.

Max is unique – jumbo-sized for a Shetland sheepdog (44 pounds instead of 24) with a jumbo personality to match.

I soon found out he was a Houdini dog — he could wiggle backward out of his harness. When I walked the two dogs I often was left holding an empty leash. I would yell, "Stay" to Mickey and chase Max down the street with no success, then turn and run so he would chase me.

When he was 7 months old, he grabbed my underwear off my leg as I was undressing and ate them. We made a trip to the emergency vet in Latham — Max as happy as a clam.

They asked, "Mrs. Shook, what kind of underwear did Max eat?"

"Purple Jockey thong," I mumbled.

"Those are very dangerous," was the reply.

If I had only known, I would have purchased the briefs.

Max was taken into an examination room. A short while later, the vet came to the lobby with the "thumbs up" sign — success, Max threw them up.

"Do you want them back?" he asked. No thanks.

Max is an active and agile dog, and we walk a lot in a beautiful land conservancy. In 2008, when I was diagnosed with breast cancer, we walked more and more. I cried on our walks, alone with Max, cried out of fear, losing my life, my family, all the fears any cancer patient knows and doesn't want to burden their friends and families with.

I was safe with Max, I knew he would comfort me. But Max was not the comforting type. He would look at me as if to say "What? You look fine – you will be fine! You are lucky, it is an early diagnosis! Now, c'mon. There is real work to do here. Squirrels to chase. Leaps to leap. Coyote poop to smell. You are wasting time."

Listen to your dogs. They tell the truth.

▶ *Contributor Norma Chepaitis Shook lives in Hudson.*

Sunny was ready to make a break for it

By Amanda Wingle

When I was a kid, my father spent many a weekend patching holes in, and otherwise reinforcing, our backyard fence. My family had a spirited yellow Lab puppy named Sunny, who had a knack for finding every possible escape route out of our backyard. A fence on our property securely confined multiple children and the dogs of friends and family for years — but Sunny was determined to break free.

There was a space between our garage and the neighbor's fence. The space seemed too narrow for a burly yellow Lab puppy to wriggle through, but Sunny found a way. After chasing her through the neighborhood for about 20 minutes and finally retrieving her, my dad devised a solution: a tall stack of cinder blocks.

One of our neighbors was a stern police officer who worked the night shift and slept through the day. My sisters and I were reminded not to make too much noise.

You can imagine our horror when, one Saturday morning, we found Sunny in that neighbor's yard. Apparently not satisfied to simply escape, she found bags of topsoil under his porch, ripped them open and dragged them all over his yard, leaving trails of dirt.

My sisters and I discussed whether to tell our parents. There seemed no way around telling them. The dog was the

Photo courtesy of Amanda Wingle

Sunny, the yellow Lab.

responsibility of my sisters and me, so after my parents rang the neighbor's doorbell and explained what happened, my sisters and I arrived with rakes, shovels and buckets to clean up what looked like a dirt explosion.

Right after Sunny passed away in 2009, during my senior year of college, I made list upon list of anecdotes about her in my journal. I never wanted to forget a single Sunny story.

Although these stories are surely amusing, the thing I remember about her above all was her sweetness and patience with my sisters and me. We were 11, 10 and 4 when we first got her. She let her human sisters dress her up in T-shirts, hats and sunglasses and never so much as growled.

She playfully stole our winter gloves right off our hands without ever touching us with an errant tooth.

She wagged her entire body, not just her tail, and the effect was similar to that of a Slinky.

We brought her on countless summer vacations to Long Beach Island, N.J., where she would accompany us to the beach and watch the seagulls and ducks.

When my grandmother developed Alzheimer's disease, Sunny was always so sweet and gentle with her. I believe she provided my grandmother with comfort.

And on the day when we had to make that difficult decision to end Sunny's suffering, she gave me the slightest wag of her tail when I came home from college to see her off to doggy heaven.

I am now 28 and when I look back on my childhood, Sunny is one of the best and most prominent parts of it.

► *Contributor Amanda Wingle lives in Albany.*

My dog who's like a cat

Drawing by Lauren Reilly

By Lauren Reilly

If I'm describing my dog Bandit, the first word that pops into my mind is "cat." You wouldn't usually describe a dog as a cat, but my dog loves cat food, despises baths and even sleeps like a cat.

Every morning, my mom wakes Bandit up. This is not as easy as it sounds. If you yell his name and say "Wake up, Bandit!" he half-opens his eyes and gives you a "why-did-you-have-to-wake-me-up" look. Once we finally persuade him to wake up, he goes downstairs, eats and reluctantly goes outside to do his business. It's likely Bandit will be back in his bed until I return from school at 2 o'clock.

The process of giving Bandit a bath is not the easiest task in the world. First, you actually have to get him in the tub. To do that, I have to pick him up and carry him up the stairs and into the bathroom, without him scurrying out the door. The actual bathing part isn't too difficult, just soap him up real good and then rinse him off.

Here comes the hard part, drying him. I have to slip out the bathroom door, grab the blow dryer and slip back in, making sure Bandit doesn't sneak out in the process. One time he escaped and by the time we caught him our floors were soaked and so were we.

My cats' food is kept in the basement. The cats are accustomed to going in and out

of the cat door. But to Bandit, the cat door is an impossible force to pass, so, when the basement is open he will seize the opportunity. Bandit sneaks down the stairs and starts to nibble at the cat food. Once his tummy is all full, he goes back upstairs like nothing happened. He might think the evidence is hidden but clearly he was mistaken when his midafternoon snack came back up. To be more clear, he barfs.

Even though adding Bandit to the family was like getting a third cat, we still love him just the same.

▶ *Contributor Lauren Reilly is a fifth-grader at Pine Bush Elementary School, Guilderland.*

My funny puppy

By Erika Para

I have a little puppy named Gerty. She is a real bozo.

I mean when I hold a treat in the air she zooms across the house until she finds that I'm holding the treat. She immediately becomes a ballerina. She stands up on her two back legs, and when I twirl with the treat in my hand, she will spin, too.

I tease her for a minute with the treat. She barks, spins and sits quietly until I give her a reward.

Sometimes, I will pull a prank on her when she sleeps. But when I call her name she doesn't respond. So I try to call her name in a deep, scary voice. She wakes up and looks at me with big eyes. Here are some things she does that makes me laugh.

She plays dead whenever she sees a squirrel, does her "business" and runs around the house.

She spills her dog food and walks out of the kitchen like nothing happened, then falls asleep on the floor.

I take Gerty and her older sister Elly for a walk. They are like our two social therapy friends Willow and Siggy. Woo-wee! They bark, play and run all day. In the wintertime, Gerty will run or bury herself in the snow. Elly, however, gives Gerty the "what are you doing, girl" look.

In the sun, Elly and Gerty attempt to "tan themselves" and I say, "You two will turn into hot dogs."

Elly runs into the house, knocks the ketchup, mustard and relish bottles off the counter, runs back outside and drops them into my hands. "My, oh my, so you want to become hot dogs?" My mom and I laugh hysterically.

Sometimes I will put a Cheez-It on Gerty's nose. She wakes up, shakes her body, sees the Cheez-It, catches it in the air and eats it.

Another time in the winter, Gerty jumped into the snow, which got on her nose and ... she sneezed. Elly got scared and ran into the house, and Gerty followed. I laughed for hours.

I realize whenever I'm sad or not happy she can cheer up a person or two.

She is very important to me. She may be 2½ years old, but she can pack quite the punch.

▶ *Contributor Erika Para is a fifth-grader at Pine Bush Elementary School, Guilderland.*

Drawing by Erika Para

Born to be in the water

By Lindsay Melanson

With my family having a pool and going to beaches and lakes a lot, Hailey had many opportunities to go swimming. Hailey was our 11-year-old golden retriever who loved to swim.

Our pool was an awesome way to let Hailey express her playful side, splashing around making a lot of waves. With a tennis ball or Frisbee and a person or two, Hailey could let her wild side show, especially when she was in the water making a commotion.

"Hailey, ready to play some fetch?" As soon as those words left my mouth, Hailey was by my side ready to race into the pool. I flung the ball into the pool with a splash! The second I gave the command, "Go get it girl!" she was off, doggy-paddling her way to the tennis ball.

Her fluffy fur coat was now matted and wet. Hailey finally retrieved the ball, but she didn't come back. She kept swimming.

"Hailey! Come on girl, can I have the ball back?"

Hailey gave me an innocent look and kept swimming. She acted like she was born to be in the water.

"Hailey, please come give me the tennis ball!"

It came to the point where my whole family was calling Hailey to come back and give us the ball. Hailey just kept pretending like we didn't exist. So, my family and I decided to continue with

Drawing by Lindsay Melanson

our day. Soon enough Hailey would notice we weren't paying attention to her. Eventually Hailey would want to join in on the fun and excitement we were having.

Time passed and Hailey was finally done swimming. Then, she came really close to me and my siblings and *shook*! Water droplets were spraying everywhere!

"Oh Hailey! You're lucky we were just about to go swimming!" I laughed.

My dog Hailey was definitely born to be in the water.

▶ *Contributor Lindsay Melanson is a fifth-grader at Pine Bush Elementary School, Guilderland.*

The excited little puppy

Drawing by Zoe Meyer

By Zoe Meyer

"Are we there yet?" I asked.

I was 5 years old when my family and I took a drive from Troy to Kansas. It was a sweaty, miserable and endless car ride but I made it "alive." The whole time my brother was screaming and crying. It was torture.

After my dad rang the doorbell I heard a number of puppies barking from the inside of the little house owned by my grandma. As my aunt opened the door, I noticed that there were numerous puppies in the arms of my grandma.

My family and I stayed for about two weeks and on the last day my dad picked out a puppy. He named him Ivan and we went back home.

When we got home he immediately adapted and started bouncing off the walls. Soon, my brother and I had to go to bed and I was really excited for tomorrow.

The next day, Ivan got his shots and my brother and I played with him all day. The day after that, we were able to take him for walks so we ended up running around dead tired. The tiny dachshund walked inside and I followed him. He started panting in front of his empty water bowl. I ran outside and asked my dad if I could refill his water bowl. I ran back outside because my dad said "yes" and I refilled it.

This was my first time so I was pretty excited that I tried something new. As I grew up so did Ivan (he's only 4 in dog years right now). One day, we went to visit our grandparents who live in Albany and that visit became a move. My dad kept Ivan at our old house, which was soon sold to another family with a dog (or two).

So, now I live at my grandparents' house and my dad lives in Pennsylvania still with Ivan, but at least he visits. Every night I lie awake for a while and think about how things have changed or that he could be in my lap right now.

Things may have changed, but not my love for Ivan.

▶ *Contributor Zoe Meyer is a fifth-grader at Pine Bush Elementary School, Guilderland.*

Finding the perfect puppy

Drawing by Alexis Mauro

By Alexis Mauro

My family was thinking of getting another dog so my dog Darius would not be alone.

A couple of days later we went to look at 3-week-old Bernese Mountain puppies. The puppies were so happy to see us. Two dogs caught my eye. I really liked the red-collared dog and the blue-collared dog but I could only get one. I was worried about picking the perfect puppy, but which pup was it?

They were so cute and fluffy. That made it harder to decide.

The breeder asked what we were looking for in a dog.

My mom said, "He should be playful, cute, fluffy and does not bite."

The breeder said, "Give me a couple of weeks and I'll find the perfect puppy for you." Then we left the breeder's house and went home.

A couple of weeks later we went back to the breeder's house and when we got there, a cute puppy was running around. He was so cute, he had a skinny white strip on his face. He has black and brown fur and brown oval patches over his eyes. He was the red-collared dog. We had the perfect name for him: Jarvis.

Jarvis was a big pup. He was the size of a medium box. The breeder said, "He is a playful pup, does not bite (that's a lie) and he is fluffy!" Sold! He was perfect.

My mom, dad and brothers took Darius and Jarvis, to meet at DiCaprio Park. They got along very well. Jarvis had completed our family. If it wasn't for the breeder helping us, we might not have found our perfect puppy.

▶ *Contributor Alexis Mauro is a fifth-grader at Pine Bush Elementary School, Guilderland.*

Oldie but a goodie

Drawing by Julia Coton

By Julia Coton

I f I had five words to describe my dog I'd choose silly, affectionate, caring, faithful and protective. If you have a dog, what five words would you pick to describe him or her?

My dog is a Chesapeake Bay retriever and her name is Kenai. Kenai's fur is a light hazel brown covered with curls. Kenai is almost 12 years old and so that means she's 77 years old in dog years! Under her chin, there's tufts of white fur that makes it look like she has a beard!!

Kenai's breed is known for how they smile like us when they're happy. That means that mostly when we're petting her, her lip curls up into a funny looking dog smile. Sometimes, you can see her pearly whites! She always makes me laugh when she smiles!

Kenai isn't just silly though, she's very protective. If a stranger approached me or my siblings, she would stand guard putting herself in between me and the stranger. Whenever she's around I always feel safe.

Every night, my brother,

sister and I take turns sleeping with her. I love sleeping with her, though sometimes you may be woken at night by her snoring! When it's your night to sleep with Kenai, you call her and she jumps up onto your bed and picks a spot next to you, or on the other end of the bed. If you're not there though when she picks her spot, then you may be sleeping on the edge of the bed!

▶ *Contributor Julia Coton is a fifth-grader at Pine Bush Elementary School, Guilderland.*

Kobe's new home

By Spencer Steinhardt

It was a Saturday afternoon and we had just won our last football game of the season. My parents had a surprise for me all along. We took a different route home than we usually go. I knew something was up. We pulled into this long driveway and my mom said, "Let's get a puppy."

There were 10 other puppies to choose from. We picked Kobe because all the other puppies were barking and nipping at our toes. Kobe was the little tiny one sleeping over in the puppy pen. We knew right away that he was the one.

When we got in the car, we all blurted out a name at the same time. So that turned out to be "glhafarafeorf." Yeah, that went over great. Finally I said, "Hey, how about Kobe?"

"That's a great one," they said. Sydney wanted to keep the original name the breeder gave him, Bobby. We also thought of Sampson for the S's in our family, but that didn't sound good. We finally agreed to call him Kobe. His full name is Kobe Sampson Mulligan Bobby Steinhardt.

Mulligan was a golf player my dad wanted to name him.

On the car ride home, Kobe was shaking badly. Sydney was holding him trying to keep him calm. As we pulled into our driveway, Kobe threw up all over Sydney. She said, "Take that dog back." Kobe ended up getting his first-ever bath right away in our kitchen sink. This was off to a rocky start, but the day got better.

Drawing by Spencer Steinhardt

Our friends knew we were getting a puppy, so they came over to meet him and brought him toys. We spent the rest of the afternoon outside.

Kobe has turned out to be the best pet my family has ever had. He is always at the door to greet us when we get home.

He lays with me when I'm sick. Somehow Kobe knows when to be gentle and when

it's time to play. Having Kobe is a big responsibility. You have to exercise him, pick up after him, entertain him and make sure he's healthy. All of this work is worth it for Kobe. He is the best dog and furry friend I could ever ask for.

▶ *Contributor Spencer Steinhardt is a fifth-grader at Pine Bush Elementary School, Guilderland.*

The golden comedian

By Nathan DeJoy

My dog is a hilarious golden retriever. Tansy is a very lazy dog when she's inside, but when she is outside, she is crazy.

When I get home from school, Tansy is calm. She is mellow, just lying around the house. When I open the back door to let her out, she becomes a dog on a sugar rush. She runs around the yard like a maniac, digging holes and barking at her friends next door. She rolls around in the grass, scratching her back, with a huge smile on her face.

Two days after we got Tansy, she ran off for three days. She probably thought we were kidnappers and she tried to set off on an adventure to find her way home. She ended up meeting several people on her journey, but when she got back home, she started to enjoy us. Whenever she got the chance, she would run down the street like a bullet. She quickly got a reputation among the neighbors that "she's a runner."

One day, Tansy just lay down in front of the back door. I kept pulling on her collar, but she stayed where she was. Tansy was fine. She was just being lazy, as usual. By the way, my dog is overweight for her age, so I really couldn't move her.

On the night of Halloween 2013, we dressed Tansy up like a horse. She had on a saddle with a rubber cowboy riding on her back. She wasn't very happy with us or the cowboy. She walked around the house very upset. Her head was hanging and I'm sure she felt embarrassed. We were laughing at the way she kept swinging the cowboy around on her back, trying to get it off.

Most of the time during the summer, Tansy uses our koi fish pond as her personal swimming pool. She chases the koi fish for a very long time, until we spot her playing in the pond and make her get out. After she gets out of the pond, she shakes herself off and water goes everywhere. I have to dry her before she comes back inside, which isn't fun. Over the winter, there is a net over the pond so Tansy can't get in. I'm sure the fish are happy not being chased around by a huge monster dog.

▶ *Contributor Nathan DeJoy is a fifth-grader at Pine Bush Elementary School, Guilderland.*

My dog Tucker

Drawing by Conner Len

By Conner Len

I have a dog and his name is Tucker as you may have guessed from the title. Tucker's favorite thing to do is to curl up into a ball, then lay down on the very top left corner of the couch.

Tucker is a breed of dog called a cocker spaniel. This type of breed has large ears like an elephant. One way I help out with Tucker is by taking him to the backyard so he can do his business.

Tucker's fur is black but because he is old, he also has little white spots everywhere. He has hazel green eyes. He's never been interested in chasing squirrels. He sneezes all the time and he loves to snuggle a lot. Tucker swims in lakes and in auntie's pool all the time. His hair grows so fast and so long that my mom has to take him to the groomer.

Tucker is so well behaved that when we go on walks in the Pine Bush, mom lets him off the leash and when we say "come" he listens. He loves to leap onto the table then eat our food. Tucker has a big under-bite, but he is still super-duper cute.

▶ *Contributor Conner Len is a fifth-grader at Pine Bush Elementary School, Guilderland.*

Eddie, the peculiar dog

Drawing by Aiden Clark

By Aiden Clark

Ever since my family adopted our terrier mutt, Eddie, he's had some peculiar behaviors. Eating wood chips and grass, which is common for a beaver, forces him to explode with vomit (nasty!). Never leaving my mom's side as if he were a toddler. Barking every time there's an animal on TV.

He's even memorized the music of the commercials with pets so he starts barking even before the animals are shown. The point is, Ed's not your typical, average, everyday dog. Whenever he's hungry, he squints at us until he has our attention and lays his paw in the food bowl. When he needs to do his business, Ed barks and points to the door with his body.

That's not all. Most people believe that dogs despise wearing clothes during the winter. Not Ed. He looks forward to the day he puts his sweater on, and loathes the day it's taken off. One day though, when he was tired of waiting, he put the sweater on himself. The sweater is very old and worn out, and I'm not looking forward to when we have to throw it in the garbage.

Another thing about Ed is that he really dislikes to be caged. No one knows exactly what happened, just that Ed somehow bent the bars to his cage. When he was put in the kennel, the only thing separating him from the rest of the kennel was a fence that didn't reach the ceiling. So, he climbed his way to freedom. Although he causes a lot of chaos and mayhem, my family and I love him anyway.

▶ *Contributor Aiden Clark is a fifth-grader at Pine Bush Elementary School, Guilderland.*

Memories with Willow

Drawing by Sanjana Stephen

By Sanjana Stephen

My best memory with Willow is when our class went snowshoeing with her. We went outside snowshoeing and Willow was ready to explode with energy.

What was so cute was when I could see little paw prints forming in a circle in the snow. Willow rolled over in the snow many times, which made her look like a fluffy snowball. She leaped and ran in the frosty snow several times. Willow always tried to cross the small rink of ice with her paws. She always ended up in a four-legged split that started skidding away. She tried to get back up, but when she did, she went flat on the ground. When the snowshoes made a big hole, Willow tried to squeeze her bottom in the hole.

She sniffed a lot of things when we took her for a walk on the trail. She sniffed things like branches, leaves and rocks. If you tried to run in her path, she would chase you around the path. Willow always looked for a spot in the snow where she could just do her own things more independently.

After the big walk, my class and I needed to go back in the classroom. Willow did not want to leave the amusing things she could do in the snow. She was hoping to have a little more Willow time in the snow. This was the best memory with Willow that I will cherish forever and keep as the most memorable activity with her.

▶ *Contributor Sanjana Stephen is a fifth-grader at Pine Bush Elementary School, Guilderland.*

Wagging tails brighten Guilderland school

By Brittany Horn

Skip Dickstein/Times Union

Labradoodle puppy Willow joins mature service dog Miss Siggy and their handlers Keith VanWagenen, fifth-grade teacher, and school social worker Catherine Ricchetti at Pine Bush Elementary School in Guilderland.

Miss Siggy wanders the halls of Pine Bush Elementary School in Guilderland, greeting students as she makes her way from classroom to classroom.

Children say she's the reason they want to come to school every day — reading time on the carpet with her is one of their favorite parts of learning. Teachers laughingly admit she's probably the cheapest employee in the district — costing about $2,500 for a lifetime of work and training — and, more than likely, the happiest to come to school every morning.

For 11 years, she's helped students face their fears, gain confidence and fall in love with education, and she's done it all without saying a word.

"She's the superhero of the school," said social worker Catherine Ricchetti. "You don't mess with Miss Siggy."

But every superhero needs a sidekick to continue her legacy, and after 11 years of service, Miss Siggy's retirement is approaching. The good news for Pine Bush students? They have two dogs to play with instead of one.

Ricchetti raised and trained Miss Siggy — short for Sigmund Freud — since the day the Goldendoodle puppy set foot in the school. What started out as her "crazy" idea has since turned into a grant-funded program that will allow the district to purchase and train five therapy dogs for its five elementary schools over the next five years.

About two weeks before Christmas, the district welcomed a fuzzy Labradoodle puppy named Willow.

In Keith VanWagenen's fifth-grade classroom, students surrounded a Buffalo Bills blanket spread on the floor. They had been reminded to put their hands behind their backs if Willow began to nip or bite at their fingers with her sharp puppy teeth.

She was 9 weeks old and still very much a puppy, but both Ricchetti and VanWagenen were firm about her training. It's the only way she'll ever learn how to be in school, Ricchetti said.

Willow moved from student to student, getting a playful rub on her back or chin. The students know if they're calm, the puppy is calm. Occasionally, Willow pounced, eliciting yelps and giggles from the students.

"We want to teach her how to be a successful therapy dog," said Julia Coton, 10.

Sydney Gonzalez, 11, said having the dog in their class makes this year extra special.

"When we grow up, we get to say we helped train her," she said. "And that's pretty cool."

▶ *This story ran in December 2014 in the Times Union.*

Red, the smelly saint, had infinite patience

By Shelby Cady

I adopted Red when she was 6 months old. She was a red bloodhound, all extra skin, ears and a deafening bay.

When my daughter was born, it was love at first sight. Celia and Red were practically inseparable, Red watching over her like a semi-comatose saint, the epitome of tolerance. She tolerated the baby gnawing on her ear, the crawler grabbing her tail and the toddler trying to ride her like the smelly (bloodhounds are incredibly smelly), groan-filled horse she thought she was.

She even proudly wore the unicorn headband around the house when Celia put it on her and called her "The Houndicorn."

Red was always super lazy, she probably slept for 20 hours a day. The only thing that could rouse her was an opportunity to eat something completely inappropriate: diapers, whole packages of baby wipes, crayons, paper towels, basically anything that had been a tree at one point in its life was fair game, as were all items within reach on the counter.

Unfortunately, I just couldn't break this awful habit. After a previous surgery to remove a rock when she was a pup, it came around again that Red had to be rushed to the vet for an obstruction.

I had her euthanized exactly five days after she

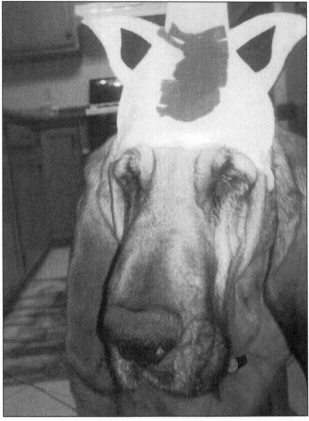

Photo courtesy of Shelby Cady

Red "The Houndicorn," a bloodhound.

started getting sick. We tried everything we could, barring a second surgery, to end her suffering, but it just didn't work. She moaned and groaned through the whole process, almost like she was still trying to fight it, bringing the vet's whole office to tears.

The hardest thing I've ever done is to go home and explain to my 2-year-old what happened to her dog. She said, "Red is my best friend" and I just held her for hours.

Celia still talks about her, four months later, how she died and now talks about death a lot. Some things will stick with a person forever even if they're only 2 years old.

▶ *Contributor Shelby Cady lives in Saratoga Springs.*

Riley is still the baby of the family

By the Diamond family

From the day we brought home Riley, our golden retriever, we knew we were in for a treat.

Riley, the "baby" of our family, was born Aug. 30, 2004, in Cairo, Greene County, and came home to Loudonville nine weeks later.

Our two sons, ages 11 and 6, had a new playmate. As a puppy, Riley was adorable and mischievous. We spent many days chasing him around the yard, trying to "steal" his tennis ball or a hat that he found.

But at 9 months, Riley seemed to lose the bounce in his step, finding it difficult to stand or run. A once-playful puppy was now too sedentary. Finally, our veterinarians diagnosed two torn ACLs and a meniscus tear in his hind legs.

The drive to Pattersonville on the morning of Riley's surgery was one of the longest and saddest of our lives. But after a long day of surgery and a day of recovery at the hospital, our Riley was home again.

Within a few months, he was back to being the fun-loving, rambunctious puppy.

However, despite his new physical strength, he could not shake his two biggest fears: thunderstorms and fireworks.

One Saturday afternoon, as Riley lay on our front lawn, a loud bang of thunder sounded. He instantly sprang up and bolted down the street like a racehorse, apparently think-

Photo courtesy of the Diamond family

Riley, a golden retriever.

ing he would be safer there. We chased after him right into our neighbors' backyard — where they were hosting a family party. Riley did end up finding a safe place there: underneath a table, at the feet of several guests. They were all very entertained by the fact that a golden retriever had crashed their party. Not even burgers and spare ribs could draw Riley out from under the table. We had to crawl under-

neath, pick him up and carry him home.

Moments like these have brought our family so much happiness and joy over the years. Now almost 11 years old, Riley is the center of our lives, and we love him more every day. No matter how sneaky he gets, he is still the "baby."

▶ *Contributors John, Cindy, Jeff and Ben Diamond live in Loudonville.*

Hunter's energy carried her through

By Debbie Lewendon

I n September 2001, shortly after 9/11, we decided our 12-year-old son, Bryan, needed a dog. We had hoped it would bring some joy and happiness into his life, as opposed to the sorrow we as a nation were feeling at the time.

We weren't quite sure what kind of dog to get, but decided on a Lab. I found a woman on the East End of Long Island who had a litter. She couldn't promise a male or female, and we had no preference, but Bryan already had a name – Hunter (named after the pro wrestler "Triple H," Hunter H. Helmsley).

One Saturday, we set off for the breeder's house. We went inside and there was Hunter, sound asleep in a large crate — the last of the litter.

The breeder let her out of the crate and off she went, running around like crazy — running into the garbage can, knocking it over, jumping all over Bryan, who was laughing with delight.

I was a little skeptical. Bryan was in love. How could we possibly leave her there now? Hunter came home with us that day.

One of her favorite things to do was take walks. Sometimes she would grab the leash in her mouth and pull us, pleading to move faster out the door. Every person and every dog in our neighborhood knew Hunter.

Over the next 10 years, Hunter had her ups and

Photo courtesy of Debbie Lewendon

The Lewendons' Labrador retriever, Hunter.

downs physically. She had to have knee surgery on both hind legs (one leg twice) and she developed cataracts that eventually took her sight.

In the summer of 2012, we learned our girl had bone cancer. We wanted what time she had to be the best it could be for her. Late summer, early fall, when the sun was warm, she would find the sunniest patch of grass and lie in it for hours.

The weekend before her last day, she must have been uncomfortable and in pain. She came over to me that Saturday night and started barking at me. I couldn't figure out why, it

was strange. Then it hit me — she was ready and was telling me, despite my broken heart, that it was time to let her go.

That Monday, a longtime friend of our family who worked for our vet came to the house and, with all of us at her side, letting her know how much we loved her, sent our girl over the rainbow bridge where I know she is waiting for us to meet again.

I cried like a baby that day. Despite being one puppy out of many, for us, she was one of a kind.

▶ *Contributor Debbie Lewendon lives in Glenmont.*

Kids loved Zack as much as he loved them

By Tami Sherry

Zack with Jessica and Michael Sherry. Top left, Tami Sherry hugs Zack. Below, Zack with Strider, the family's other dog.

Zack was a husky/Lab mix we found while visiting friends in the Catskills in the middle of February. He fit right in once he was accepted by our resident shepherd mix. He never needed a leash and should have been called Shadow — he followed me everywhere. When the children arrived, he adored them. He slept between their bedrooms every night. He happily accepted all other dogs and children and became a favorite of the neighborhood children due to his charming personality. He was always with the children in the yard, napped with the babies, sat perfectly still for story time and loved car rides.

As Zack got older, the children worried. He lost his hearing and hated missing the doorbell, feeling as if he wasn't doing his job properly.

When he had some small strokes, it became time to talk about letting him go. Every child in the neighborhood cried and came to a goodbye party. We bathed him, brought him out into the sun and all the kids paid their respects. Then we let him go.

We've never gotten another dog, even though we'd had many before, because he was simply the best dog ever.

▶ *Contributor Tami Sherry lives in Albany.*

A dog in a baby carriage? That's Hunter

By Allison Jeffers

Before my husband and I were married, he told me he never wanted a dog. However, 10 years later he changed his tune. I was a stay-at-home mom of two boys and the only thing missing was a dog.

Off we went to a puppy adoption clinic at a local pet store. We were running late so I went up by myself and my husband and boys were going to meet me there.

As I pulled up, a woman was standing at the back of her SUV with a large dog crate. Inside I could see quite a few small sleepy golden retriever-looking puppies. As I yelled to the woman to find out if she was coming or going, a black-and-tan coonhound's head popped up over the bunch.

I knew at that moment that was my dog. We brought him home that day.

We named him Hunter and he was a very good puppy. He learned commands quickly and trained very easily. He loved being outside. If we weren't out walking, he was outside on his lead but only in the front yard. He didn't like to be in the backyard.

A month later, my older son, Brendan, started school. Every morning, I put my younger son, Michael, in the carriage, leashed the dog and walked to the bus stop. We took a walk after the bus left and headed home. I put Hunter on the lead, took Michael

Photos courtesy of Allison Jeffers

Hunter, a black and tan coonhound.

into the house and left the carriage out there to use for our afternoon walk to pick up Brendan. Hunter sat on the lawn for hours, basking in the sun.

One chilly fall day, Hunter proved how much he loved being outside. We followed our normal routine and after a while I looked outside to check on him. I could see the lead but not Hunter.

A little panicked, I quickly went outside to find Hunter had climbed into the carriage to stay warm. He stayed in there all morning. This new routine continued until the winter, even after the first snowfall.

People would stop in disbelief that a dog was sitting in a carriage. He would just sit there and look at them like it was perfectly normal. Even the school bus would slow down as it passed my house so the kids could look at the dog in the carriage.

My husband never regretted getting a dog. We had to put Hunter down after 14 years. He was a true family dog and there is quite a void without him here. We miss him very much.

▶ *Contributor Allison Jeffers lives in Loudonville.*

Ray's loyalty overcame his quirky nature

By Dan Doyle

When I was first introduced to Raymond G. Shepherd in October 1995, he was just over a year old and had already been through two owners.

He was the most beautiful dog I'd ever seen – a goofy, playful animal bounding all over Pinebush Kennels with a giant smile, shattering every stereotype I'd held about how German shepherds should behave. Against any sort of judgment, I walked off with him that day, and the only instruction I received as I took the leash and headed for the door was, "Ray needs a lot of love."

From the day I brought Ray home, he followed me to every room and cried if I left his line of vision for even a moment.

Ray was a 100-pound force of nature, and he quickly took it upon himself to defend me from anyone he deemed a threat, which was nearly everyone. While I generally witnessed these protective episodes from behind, I know that angry Ray, dancing, with growling face contorted in rage, was terrifying. Never once did he growl at a child.

But Ray was also an absolute charmer, and almost unbelievably gentle. Those who were his favorites can probably still picture him charging up, ears pinned back and tail swinging in circles. He had as much of a sense of humor as can be ascribed to a dog, and lived to coax the fun side out of people.

Photo courtesy of Dan Doyle

Raymond G. Shepherd as a young dog.

Early on, Ray suffered from severe separation anxiety. About a month into our relationship, I left Ray in my Honda Accord and returned to discover he had destroyed the interior. After our veterinarian suggested I crate Ray when leaving the house, the dog somehow managed to hop the crate across the room, pull my down comforter through the bars, and shred it. I will never forget coming home to find that dog, in the middle of a feather-filled bedroom, genuinely thrilled to see me.

He later managed to bend the steel bars on a friend's kennel with his teeth while I was traveling. Two men, working simultaneously, were unable to bend the bars back into place.

He once managed to switch on a gas stove burner while I was out, nearly starting a fire.

It's worth noting that none of the items destroyed matter at all to me now and Ray still does.

The fact that Ray was able to turn doorknobs with his teeth and escape from a variety of attempts to contain him made these situations difficult to avoid.

As challenging as the early years were, Raymond was the best dog a person could ever wish for. Over the years, he followed me to nine addresses, outlasted four cars and shared a roof at various times with nine house mates, seven cats and one other dog.

In the end, I came to realize that Ray was so easy for me to love because he was me. His constant pacing, his anxiety, his desire to do the right thing only to get it so consistently and utterly wrong ... he and I just got each other.

▶ *Contributor Dan Doyle lives in Delmar.*

Sox loved Oreos and milk

By Kelly Hallenbeck

As I sit here reminiscing back to my childhood days with my best four-legged friend Sox, I crave Oreo cookies and milk.

It was our after-school ritual. He knew the very minute I went to the cookie jar and there he'd sit at full attention.

Mom's limit to my sister and me was always four cookies. It was an unwritten "cookie-limit rule," still an inside joke even though we're in our 40s.

Sox always knew that by the time I got down to the last half of that fourth cookie, well, that was his moment. The drool was almost hitting the floor by then. He'd waited so patiently. I'd dunked the first half of my fourth cookie in my milk, bitten off my half, then he finally got what he waited for. He enjoyed that half of an Oreo as if it were a T-bone steak.

I'd finish my milk, pet him approvingly and he'd go carry off his favorite kitchen towel and lie back down.

He just had this thing for sucking and biting on kitchen towels. It was a strange habit, started not long after he was rescued by my dad.

My dad found Sox in a snowbank on his way home from work. Sox was between 4 and 6 weeks old. My dad came home with him tucked inside his winter coat. I was only 8 years old.

I don't really remember how he got a hold of his first kitchen towel, but once he did, he never let go. He'd just lie there and suck on it like it was a huge cloth pacifier. He had a pretty

Photo courtesy of Kelly Hallenbeck

Bailey, the new dog in Kelly Hallenbeck's life.

sizable collection. It was hilarious. If you laughed at him, he'd just stop for a minute, keep the towel in his mouth, look at you with those brown eyes as if he were saying, "You do know I'm right here don't you?"

I think it was because he had no chance to wean. Whatever it was, it was Sox's trademark.

Sox was just the very best dog. At Christmastime one year, I can remember he let me string garland all around him and paint his nails red and wait for my parents to get home from work.

So many Kelly and Sox stories really ... 15 years worth. Then the age began to show. His legs became weak. My dad helped him as needed. But the incontinence started and it was inevitable. It was time to say goodbye to Sox.

Dad wouldn't let any of us go with him. It was kind of poetic.

It began with just him and Sox, it should end that way, too.

To this day, I still think of Sox with the second dunk of that fourth Oreo cookie. Kitchen towels are still a funny reminder of his little quirky habit, which means I'll never have to completely say a final goodbye to him.

I cannot advocate enough for rescuing a dog. I've now rescued a dog in my adulthood. His name is Bailey and he's basically rescued me. It's completely different but somehow just the same as having a dog as a child.

I think Sox would really like Bailey. But, don't worry, Sox, Oreos and milk will always be our special snack. Bailey's more of a popcorn and carrots kind of guy.

▶ *Contributor Kelly Hallenbeck lives in Stuyvesant.*

Jake, a lifetime pooch

By Kim Kendrick

As the owner of a professional dog-grooming salon, I have several friends and clients who are counting the days for their very sick and very elderly dogs. I can't help but to empathize with them, of course, but don't count so fast.

In Jon Katz's book "A Good Dog," he talks about Orson, his "lifetime dog." It's a special kind of relationship between a man and his dog. If you haven't read it, you might want to. If you have, you'll understand when I say my beagle Jake was my lifetime dog.

I got Jake as a puppy in North Carolina. I was 22, and my father had helped me move, bought me a few things for my apartment and told me that, financially, I was on my own. I bought a small truck and realized every truck needs a dog.

I rescued my dog from a farmer who was unable to care for him and his siblings. He was the runt and so stinkin' cute. And stinky. I cleaned him up and moved to New York.

Jake was given a death sentence a few times in his life. He was a sick little boy on and off for a couple years, but his conditions were manageable and he was a happy dog.

One night, he collapsed suddenly in severe pain and an emergency X-ray found a baseball-sized tumor on his spleen. I was told by the emergency vet they would give him pain meds to get him through the night, but that he'd have to be put down the next day. It was a long, tearful night, but the next day, his regular vet said not to

Photo courtesy of Kim Kendrick

Jake the beagle with Kim Kendrick's son.

rush the decision.

It turned out the pain was from acute pancreatitis, not cancer. The tumor was a coincidental find. Once he was better, the tumor was removed and he did great.

More than a year later, Jake stopped eating and drinking. An aggressive cancer had spread to his stomach and other areas, and he needed to be euthanized before he starved to death. I wanted his regular vet to do it, so we made an appointment for the next day. I said my goodbyes.

I put our son to bed that night and stepped outside to cry so he wouldn't hear me.

I woke up in the morning and Jake ate breakfast. I always say he must have been thinking, "Holy you-know-what, she's serious! I better quit fooling around!" My wonderful vet said maybe today wasn't his day. And neither were the next 500 days.

I kept taking Jake to the vet every few months just to show him Jake was still chugging along. He said to me many times that he could offer no explanations of why Jake was still alive and that I should be thankful every day.

And I was.

It wasn't until Nov. 4, 2009, at 14½ years old, that Jake snuggled in bed with our son for the last time. We awoke to find him in distress, and we knew his time had run out.

I told him over and over how sorry I was that I was choosing to end his life. But looking back, I know what I really gave him was a gift of peace, and an end to his suffering. After all of the times he helped me, it was the least I could do.

The time dogs give us is unmeasured and the love they give is unparalleled. Lap it up.

▶ *Contributor Kim Kendrick lives in Latham.*

Watching the birds

"Dogs are our link to paradise. They don't know evil or jealousy or discontent. To sit with a dog on a hillside on a glorious afternoon is to be back in Eden, where doing nothing was not boring— it was peace."

— Milan Kundera

Photo courtesy of Joanne Lue

Joanne Lue's grandson Kellen says goodbye to his friend Jake the boxer.

By Joanne Lue

I enjoyed many glorious afternoons with my boxer Jake during his 12 years.

For us it was sitting in the sun on the deck watching birds at the feeder. I miss those moments in "Eden" with Jake by my side.

▶ *Contributor Joanne Lue lives in Guilderland.*

A love for stinky cheese and blonde women

By Denis Meadows

Scout was our first dog. My wife and I had not yet decided to get a dog when, in May 2003, she returned from a Peppertree Rescue adoption clinic with Scout. She went to the adoption clinic to get information; she returned with so much more.

Scout selected my wife, and came to our Delmar home for a two-week trial period. The trial period lasted more than 10 years — we welcomed Scout into our hearts and home.

He arrived as a striking yet scared 2-year-old husky-Great Pyrenees-cocker spaniel mutt. He had the fluffy coat of a Great Pyrenees, the red-and-white color of a husky and the floppy ears of a cocker spaniel. He was smaller than that combination would suggest, never weighing more than 50 pounds.

Scout was afraid of men, but he loved the ladies. His original family included three blonde girls and he was always drawn to blondes. It was more than two weeks before Scout accepted me and let me pet him.

As a young dog, Scout was full of energy. We chased each other in the backyard before and after work, we let him run off-leash at Partridge Run Preserve and there was the occasional "jail break" where he would be high-stepping it down our street only to be lured back with the promise of cheese. He even had a brief stint running agility with my wife, until physical limitations put an end

Photo courtesy of Denis Meadows
Scout, a husky-Great Pyrenees-cocker spaniel mix.

to his agility career.

After 10 years of marriage, my wife and I separated. We had three dogs — two purebred, athletic golden retrievers and Scout. I kept Scout, the lovable oaf of a dog, and my wife kept the goldens. Scout had long ceased to be my wife's dog and always preferred being an only dog.

In June of 2013, Scout was diagnosed with cancer. A tumor had developed on his right front paw and the vet gave us two options — really, one. It was clear to both me and the vet that there would be no radiation, there would be no surgery. I would do nothing, other than make Scout's remaining time comfortable and enjoyable.

The next few months, Scout's health gradually declined, but his goofy grin and wagging tail remained constant. As he struggled to get into his favorite chair, I

removed the feet so he could climb in on his own. When the deck stairs became a challenge, a dog agility A-frame became a makeshift ramp. The hardwood floors were covered in area rugs so Scout could make his way from room to room.

By late December, Scout could no longer support himself and I knew it was time.

Scout and I spent most of the weekend together. I slept on the living room floor with him. That Monday, my wife and I reunited to say goodbye to Scout.

At 13, he was no longer young and scared, but he still loved the ladies. He had developed a taste for bacon, chicken and stinky cheese.

We said goodbye to Scout knowing we had given him the best life and he had given us so much more.

▶ *Contributor Denis Meadows lives in Delmar.*

Cassidy Bono, the best dog ever

By Silvia Meder Lilly

'␣ve been thinking that, for me, dogs are kind of like Christmas trees. They're special and they make a house feel like a home.

Each year, when we get our tree decorated and beautifully lit, I think to myself, "This is the best tree ever." It's the same with the dogs with whom I have been lucky enough to share a home – each one has been the "best dog ever." That thought makes me smile.

Cassidy is the dog my children will always know as their first pet. She arrived a ball of black fluff and quickly determined that the best way to make her mark was to be the mellow one in a house chaotic with both a toddler and a 4-year-old.

Her full name, Cassidy Bono, came from my choice for a girl's name during my second pregnancy and the fact that we went to see U2 the night before we picked her up from the breeder.

She loved her boys and would happily share their beds, clean up their Cheerios, and leap off the dock to land in the water beside them.

She was my cross-country skiing buddy for a decade – never protesting when I wanted to go the extra distance. One winter, she ended up in the Normans Kill after a very heavy and powdery snowstorm. I took my skis off, got down on my belly and yanked her out of the frigid water, wag-

Photo courtesy of Silvia Meder Lilly

Cassidy with Silvia Meder Lilly's son Quinn.

ging her tail all the while.

We finished our loop of the golf course, pausing as necessary to knock the balls of frozen snow off her belly. She was such a great companion.

We learned that she had a tumor, probably malignant. Our veterinary practice, Boght Animal Hospital in Latham, as always, gave us compassionate and pragmatic advice — take her home, feed her anything she wants to eat and love her. We did.

She enjoyed these last days, eating pork shoulder, sirloin steak, chicken breast and holiday turkey. And biscuits, lots of biscuits.

On her last day with us, Cassidy wouldn't walk down

the stairs. I sat on the floor next to her, my tears dripping on the softest fur a dog has ever had.

She looked me in the eyes and I knew. It was time and, like she always did, she made it easy.

I called the vet. When we arrived, there was a soft patchwork blanket on the floor and she immediately lay down.

She was tired and I could hear her telling me it was OK. I'd like to think that the last thing she heard was my voice telling that she was a good girl and that I loved her.

She was the best dog ever.

▶ *Contributor Silvia Meder Lilly lives in Albany.*

Simba the lion was king of the house

By Clare Mertz

The kids and I piled into the car and drove to Menands "just to look" at the shelter dogs available for adoption. We went in looking for a younger dog, not necessarily a puppy, but maybe one age 1 to 3.

The dogs barked and yelped and jumped and ran, each seeking to get our attention: big ones, little ones, fat ones, thin ones, all different colors, all different types. And then we saw Simba.

He was 8. He calmly wagged his tail. My eyes locked on his. This was my dog. I knew it. He did, too.

I found out that he was being treated for Lyme disease.

I walked down the row and gave the other dogs a look. 8 years old? Lyme disease? I saw two women come in from a rescue shelter and walk toward his cage. I couldn't bear to watch that calm, sweet dog with the fluffy tail and smiling, wise face leave me. "I want him," I thought.

Simba was not good on a leash. He pulled me all over the street. He ran around the play yard and didn't give me or the kids another look. They checked our references, got the pills together, and we paid a much-reduced adoption fee due to his age and special needs.

The car door opened and in he leapt. He ran all over and nuzzled the delighted kids. His hair was flying every-

Photo courtesy of Clare Mertz

Simba, a Lab/chow mix.

where and I thought, "I had better get a better vacuum — a Shop Vac!"

Simba the lion was ours, the Lab/chow mix who loved everyone, who howled when he did not get his way, who loved toys and making messes, who had his own daily dog walker and who would walk for miles if you let him. One time, I drove into the neighborhood and saw a dog that looked just like him strolling down the street and a police car in my driveway because the neighbors were concerned that someone must have broken in since the dog was never out alone.

It was Simba.

For 5½ years he was the king of the bed, sprawled out so that we had to tuck ourselves around him. He tracked in mud, brought me dead bird presents, rolled over something rotten so that it was enmeshed in his thick coat, counter surfed, swam in the pond and shook the water all over us, and exuberantly loved every person with whom he came into contact.

Simba the great, king of the bed, lord of everything malodorous — a dog among dogs.

▶ *Contributor Clare Mertz lives in Voorheesville.*

Rosie is the center of her family's universe

Rosie's family: Alyssa, Matt and Maria Potvin.

Photo courtesy of Maria Potvin

By Maria Potvin

Rosie brings so much joy to our home. She wants nothing more than to love and be loved.

Rosie is the center of so much of our family time. We often say, "What did we do before we adopted Rosie?" It is incredible how quickly she became the center of our world.

Rosie bonds with her "sister," Alyssa, by playing hide and seek around the house. (Alyssa hides and Rosie seeks). Rosie leaves no stone unturned when she is trying to find her sister. While we say, "Where is your sister? Where is Alyssa?" She is looking behind the couch, under chairs and in places so small there is no way Alyssa could be there.

When Rosie eventually finds Alyssa, she wags her tail with such excitement that her entire bottom half is moving back and forth (her "wiggle butt").

When Rosie isn't playing hide and seek, she can be found destroying toys. Upon receiving a new toy, she uses her incredibly strong teeth to dissect the toy and present the stuffing to us as a gift.

Her rope toys seem to take quite a bit longer to destroy and are her staple. As soon as one of us arrives home, she runs to get her rope toy and drops it at our feet to play tug of war, fetch or to simply guard the rope toy so we can't grab it from her.

Rosie is our little Snuggle Monster, Love Bug, Frito Feet, Rosebud, daughter and sister all rolled into a one-of-a-kind terrier mix.

▶ *Contributor Maria Potvin lives in Castleton-on-Hudson.*

Suzy the rottweiler was Mom's guardian

By Regina Ruede

We have had and still have many amazing dogs in our lives, but Suzy, our Rottweiler, was an example of unconditional love and protection.

Rotties are known for their protective nature, but they are often perceived as vicious dogs because of that very nature.

My mom's health was failing fast at 81 years old. It became clear that we needed to find a home where she would be safe and well cared for. She lived on Long Island and we lived upstate, so she asked if she could live with us.

Family and friends were concerned because we owned a large Rottweiler along with two small shelties.

Before we moved Mom in, we had our Rottie evaluated. It was determined that dogs like her needed a job. She was loving and gentle, but no one dared to enter our little farm while Suzy was on duty.

Mom moved in and the most amazing thing happened: Suzy and Mom bonded.

We expected that Mom would be lonely coming from a busy city life to our little hobby farm, but by bonding with our Suzy, Mom found a friend who would love her unconditionally and Suzy found the job she needed. She would sit with Mom for hours as Mom stroked her velvety ears.

She became Mom's dog.

Many health care profes-

Photo courtesy of Regina Ruede
Suzy, the Rottweiler, with Regina Ruede's mother, Dorothy.

sionals came and went during the two years Mom was with us. Some wanted the dogs to be locked up and others understood that the animals were part of the family. We always acted on the side of caution to protect both the visitors and the dogs' reputations, but one visiting nurse ordered that we keep that Rottweiler away from my mom.

My mom and I told her that it is not my mom who would be in danger, the danger would be for anyone who looks like they might hurt my mom.

During my mom's last two weeks, she needed 24-hour care. We got an Army cot so I could sleep in her bedroom to attend to her, but Suzy had a different idea. She was sure that cot was for her and she would share it with me if I had to stay, too. She made us laugh when we needed it most.

When Mom passed, Suzy showed signs of depression. Luckily, dogs live in the here and now and before you knew it, she was back to her old tricks of stealing tissues and snacks off the table.

Suzy passed just a year and half after my mom.

I imagine that Mom is in heaven with Suzy beside her and she is getting those heavenly velvet ears stroked. They were meant to be together.

▶ *Contributor Regina Ruede lives in Altamont.*

Griffin's heart was as big as his stature

By Alicia Soper

I t would have been impossible for me to predict the profound impact that a dog can have on a person's life.

Our beloved Irish wolfhound Griffin passed away in October 2013, and while his presence may no longer be felt, the hole in our hearts and the tears that fall during nostalgic moments are very real.

Griffin was 200 pounds of stoic grandeur, standing 36 inches at the shoulder. From his arrival at 13 weeks old to his departure from this Earth much too soon at 6½, he was a bit of a local celebrity in our small village of Dolgeville, Herkimer County.

Our daily walks allowed many to join us in the joy of watching him grow from a goofy, awkward puppy to the larger-than-life handsome gray beast that was an amazing presence in our lives and tremendous source of pride.

He was the dog we wanted, researched, raised and loved. We were proud of Griffin for many reasons. While his size may have intimidated some, he was always respectful and friendly to anyone he met, human or animal. I have heard people talk of animals having a sixth sense, or the ability to understand a person's needs, and we saw this in Griffin's gentle manner and the kindness in his eyes that he seemed to reserve for people in our village who may have

Photo courtesy of Alicia Soper

Alicia Soper with her Irish wolfhound, Griffin.

needed that bit of love and understanding in their lives.

Griffin was devoted to our family of two, the extent of which I was not fully aware of until his passing. I usually arrive home from work an hour or so after my husband. Griffin would faithfully signal my impending arrival into our driveway by standing at the window and occasionally letting out a short, low timbre bark, but mostly he would stand.

The first indicators of his fading health were evident in his struggle to come to all fours, a duty he assigned to himself, and faithfully executed until he could no longer.

It will be two years in

October that Griffin has been gone. The sound of his "let me in!" woof occasionally rings in our ears, though it has grown more faint, as has the sound of his massive frame settling in his bed for a good night's sleep, a sound I was most fond of and took great comfort in.

Griffin is missing from our home, but is forever in our memories. We have continued to be endlessly entertained by our wirehaired dachshund, Tederich, and our most recent additions, greyhounds Fiona and Blue. There is just something special in the heart of a hound.

▶ *Contributor Alicia Soper lives in Dolgeville, Herkimer County.*

The king of Buckingham

By Elmer Streeter

On Saturday, Sept. 1, 2001, we brought home an adorable male German shepherd puppy.

The breeder chose that particular puppy for us because she said he was "going to be a big one" and thought I would be able to handle him.

We named him Kaiser Von Buckingham Streeter — "King of Buckingham" — after the pond we live near. Kaiser was so small at the time he could hide under the coffee table, but not for long.

Kaiser grew into a very big boy, weighing nearly 100 pounds — a true gentle giant.

Kaiser was an incredible family dog and the greatest friend to me. We took walks almost every night. He was a great walker — on and off the leash. We cherished this time together.

Kaiser was the most considerate listener to all the problems I had. He helped me make some tough decisions and helped me through some difficult times. I am a much better person because of him.

Kaiser went everywhere with us when he was younger, choosing not to as he got older. He loved to play ball, proudly bringing the ball back every time, for as long as we would continue to throw it.

My kids used to give me grief that I had more pictures of Kaiser than them in my office, but the truth is my kids gave me most of those photos.

From the time he was 7 months old, Kaiser was "Mr. Calm" but with a worried

Photo courtesy of Elmer Streeter

Kaiser Von Buckingham Streeter, the "King of Buckingham," named after the Albany neighborhood pond.

look. He was a gentle dog, but protective. His size and bark were a warning to all. He loved Sarge, my daughter Heather and her husband Chris' dog, and our other German shepherd, Kiera.

In 10 years and 7 months, Kaiser only broke my heart once — on April 6, 2012, when I held him lovingly at home while the vet put him to sleep, surrounded by the people Kaiser loved so much.

He died with the great dignity he lived with. He died without pain, in the house that he loved and that he hated to leave except for walks.

Kaiser had a great life. We had a great love. It was a real privilege to have him as part of our family.

▶ *Contributor Elmer Streeter lives in Albany.*

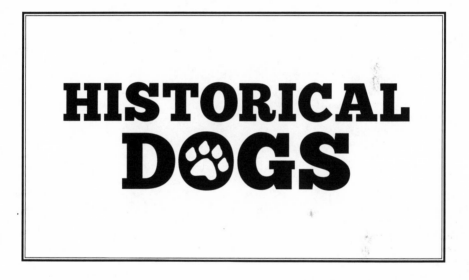

HISTORICAL DOGS

Many dogs called
Executive Mansion home

By Paul Grondahl

Photo courtesy of AllPosters.com

Thomas E. Dewey Jr., the governor's son, guides his dog's jump.

As midnight approached each night in the darkened Executive Mansion in the mid-1950s, Gov. W. Averell Harriman was long asleep in his bedroom when his wife, Marie, made a ritual trip downstairs from an adjoining bedroom.

The first lady carried her ever-present companions, wire-haired dachshunds Andine and Gary Cooper, one under each arm like bundles of firewood, down the ornately carved grand staircase.

The governor's dog, Brum, a yellow Labrador retriever who slept outside Harriman's bedroom door, was awakened by the sound and lumbered along at the first lady's heels.

A night owl who routinely slept until 11 o'clock or noon in her private boudoir while her workaholic husband arose at 6 a.m., Marie Harriman retreated in the wee hours each night to the kitchen to talk with a trooper on duty, old Sergeant Gilmore. The dachshunds slept on her lap, the Lab lolled at her feet and they swapped stories as she drank two bottles of Whitbread Ale.

When someone tried to slip in a Genesee beer the company sent to the mansion, she opined: "Tastes like cow's piss."

The second wife of the Groton-educated scion of a railroad fortune, she and Harriman were married for 40 years, until her death in 1970. Marie Harriman was known for her stylish attire, including pearls and mink coat, and she shared her husband's passion for collecting art. She had a personal maid she paid for privately, who traveled with her and the dogs between the governor's mansion and Harriman's homes in New York City and Arden, Orange County.

A heavy cigarette smoker with an earthy sense of humor, the first lady hosted teas and soirees for garden clubs and ladies' groups at the mansion, and confided to friends that she was lonely in the sprawling, 41-room historic mansion on Eagle Street. Her dachshunds were her constant companions.

Historical footnote: Her husband was the only governor who had a dog — his beloved Brum, seated at Harriman's knee — included in his official portrait that hangs in the Hall of Governors on the second floor of the state Capitol.

"Mrs. Harriman's greatest love was her dogs. She brought Andine and Gary Cooper everywhere with her and they especially loved to go on rides in the car," said Robert Bennett, who came to the Executive Mansion at the age of 23 in 1953 as butler and valet for Gov. Thomas E. Dewey. He retired in 1991 as superintendent who served six governors: Thomas Dewey, Harriman, Nelson Rockefeller, Malcolm Wilson, Hugh Carey and Mario Cuomo.

Dogs were a recurring theme with New York's first families, even before Bennett arrived at 138 Eagle St. more than 60 years ago.

Gov. Al Smith loved animals and he received so many creatures as gifts during his four terms that he had the mansion's grounds converted into a zoo in the early 1920s. He filled the property with a menagerie that included monkeys and a bear cub.

Smith's favorite animals were his Great Danes, Cesar and Jeff. "Gov. Al Smith is a great dog fancier," Dog Fancier magazine reported in 1919. "His Great Dane, Cesar, is one of the largest dogs in America. Cesar will guard the Executive Mansion. Smith is also very keen on Boston terriers and considers them the champion bantam breed of the dog world."

Cesar was so big he could leap the wrought-iron fence and he was also known to slip through an open gate. Another of the governor's Great Danes with Houdini-like skills was named Jeff, who made a headline-making breakout on April 6, 1924.

The Times Union headline: "Pshaw! The Kids Had a Corker Of A Dog Till The Cops Came."

Little Eddie Morrissey of Main Street, a plucky 10-year-old lad, rode around on the back of Jeff as if he were a pony until police spotted the rogue li'l jockey and runaway dog. They pulled the boy off the massive canine and returned Jeff to the Executive Mansion. "Little Eddie was left behind open mouthed and sorrowful at the strange events of the morning," the Times Union reported. "Perhaps he did not know that the whole city was on the lookout for that particular dog."

The first dog Bennett shared the mansion with in the 1940s was Gov. Thomas Dewey's pet, a large, brown standard poodle whose name he could not recall. "Governor Dewey would come home from the Capitol each night and feed his dog, who stood up on his hind legs and was as tall as a door," Bennett recalled. "That dog was always hungry."

Bennett said the mansion's chef and kitchen staff liked to spoil the pets of governors, including Gov. Nelson Rockefeller's cat, which was a gift. "Governor Rockefeller was doing a bridge dedication in Kingston and a little boy had two kittens he was trying to give away and the governor said he'd take one," Bennett recalled. "He ended up calling it Happy."

When Rockefeller left the governorship in 1973 after four terms, Happy the cat remained at the mansion. "Happy was never a problem. The kitchen staff took good care of her," Bennett said.

Gov. Hugh Carey arrived at the Capitol recently widowed in 1974 and the six youngest of his 12 children lived in the governor's mansion, with a lot of help from the staff. Bennett's wife, Noreen, was a schoolteacher who helped the Carey kids with homework. Bennett helped deal with any issues that arose at the children's schools.

The most rambunctious member of the Carey brood was Jet, a spirited black Labrador retriever. Jet loved to dig holes under the mansion's metal fence and slip past State Police troopers on duty at the gate. Generally, the city's dog warden would quickly catch and return the fugitive Lab before he wandered too far.

"One day, Jet got loose and was gone for a long time. I thought he was a goner," Bennett recalled. "The kids were very upset."

Bennett called the local dog shelters, but they had not taken in a black Lab. He placed a classified ad in the Times Union. Several days later, the Carey dog was brought to the Mohawk Hudson Humane Society in Menands and the staff called Bennett.

"The kids were very happy to have Jet back," Bennett said.

Perhaps the best-known governor's dog of recent decades was Gov. Mario M. Cuomo's mixed-breed terrier, Ginger, who lived a charmed life in the mansion. It was his son Christopher's dog when he attended The Albany Academy, but stayed behind when his son left home for Yale University in 1988. Ginger became the governor's ever-present companion. Chris went on to become a celebrity TV personality, currently with CNN.

"Ginger was very faithful to Governor Cuomo," Bennett recalled. "Ginger would sit by the governor like a little guard dog as he wrote for hours in his study."

Ginger was a frequent topic on Cuomo's weekly radio show, the "Capital Connection" on WAMC-FM with host Alan

Chartock. The 30-minute show featured playful banter and Cuomo's trademark wit, along with making Chartock the butt of his running jokes. When the repartee turned to Ginger, Cuomo needled Chartock about his looks and often referred to the radio host as "a fire hydrant with a necktie."

Cuomo turned introspective and wistful as Ginger became ill and died in 1991. "Ginger is dying," Cuomo read from his diary on the radio show, which drew thousands of listeners in five states. "Could we have treated Ginger better?"

Chartock recounted the segment in his book, "Me and Mario."

"Every animal owner's heart melted when he spoke about Ginger dying," Chartock wrote.

The segment was replayed and became a donor premium in subsequent years on WAMC fundraisers.

A few months after Ginger's death, Cuomo's son Andrew, the current governor, brought his father an 8-week-old German shepherd as a present on Christmas Eve, 1991.

Cuomo suggested they call the puppy Ginger, but his family nixed that, he told reporters. He suggested Ninja, because the dog "looked Japanese" and it sounded like his beloved Ginger.

The family said no. They also turned thumbs down on Binger.

Finally, Cuomo came up with Cara. It means "dear one" in Italian and reminded the governor of an old song that begins, "Cara mia..."

Photo courtesy of New York Executive Chamber

The official state portrait of Gov. William Averell Harriman (1891-1986), shown with his dog, Brum. The painting hangs in the Hall of Governors in Albany.

"It's perfect," Cuomo said. This time, his family agreed.

Cara the puppy grew up in the Executive Mansion and was spoiled by Cuomo. Even as a full-grown dog of 75 pounds, the governor allowed Cara to plop her large front paws on his lap as he sat at a kitchen table early each morning and enjoyed a bagel for breakfast.

He was known to slip Cara table scraps.

Cara left the only home she knew with her master on Dec.

31, 1994, at the conclusion of Cuomo's third term, following his defeat to Republican gubernatorial candidate George E. Pataki.

Cara was the last dog to live full-time in the Executive Mansion.

Cuomo died on Jan. 1, 2015, following complications from a heart condition. He was 82.

▶ *pgrondahl@timesunion. com* ▪ *518-454-5623* ▪ *@PaulGrondahl*

Humane Society's roots in 19th century

By Paul Grondahl

T he roots of the Mohawk Hudson Humane Society stretch back more than a century, making it among the earliest organizations of its kind in the country, although it initially had nothing to do with dogs and cats.

It was founded in 1887 as the Albany County Society for the Prevention of Cruelty to Children, prompted by a case of a girl born in the county poorhouse.

The group's earliest headquarters were in West Troy and its operations included cases of animals as well as children in Albany and Rensselaer counties. In 1892, the name was changed to the Mohawk and Hudson River Humane Society for the Prevention of Cruelty to Animals. Two years later, the state Legislature passed a law that officially made the local group the first combined society in New York state.

In 1897, the group, with the help of city officials, built a shelter for children in Troy. In 1901, a similar children's shelter was built in Albany.

In 1903, the agency received 378 children and cared for them for 3,181 days.

A guiding force in the organization's early development was Dr. William O. Stillman, a physician and professor at Albany Medical College, who specialized in treating infants and children. He also helped found the Open Door Mission and Hospital for Incurables in

Photo courtesy of the Mohawk Hudson Humane Society
The entrance to the Humane Society on Fourth Street in Troy.

Albany in 1887.

He rescued the Albany society from financial dire straits when he became president of the local group in 1892. He took over an organization that had no office, no supplies, no paid employees and only a few hundred dollars in the bank. He moved operations into a building at Eagle and Jay streets in downtown Albany, which became popularly known as the Humane Society building. He was also a major financial supporter of its work.

Stillman was assisted by fellow dog lover Bishop William Croswell Doane of the Episcopal Cathedral of All Saints. Doane walked around Albany with his constant companion, a St. Bernard named Cluny. Doane's dog was the only one allowed into the Capitol and the governor's executive chamber.

Stillman presented a picto-

rial history of the Mohawk and Hudson River Humane Society at the 1904 World's Fair Exposition in Saint Louis, Mo., where he received a gold medal for philanthropic services.

Stillman often investigated cases of animal abuse and cruelty himself. He became deeply moved after reading stories of animals pressed into duty during World War I. That led him to join forces with the American Red Star Animal Relief effort, similar to the Red Cross, which raised money and awareness about animals mistreated in the war.

In 1913, the Mohawk Hudson Humane Society moved to its present home at 3 Oakland Ave., off Broadway, in Menands. The estate of William Van Rensselaer gave 15 acres to the organization for $1 and the deed included a stipulation that Van Rensselaer descendants would be free to walk the property whenever they wished and that the organization would not open a tavern or sell alcohol on the property. The original barn still stands at the site.

Also in 1913, Stillman became the founding editor of the National Humane Review, a periodical that focused on child and animal abuse cases across the country and reform legislation on animal issues.

Stillman's passionate leadership was credited with increasing the number of local anti-cruelty societies across the U.S. from 280 in 1904 to 565 in 1924.

In 1923, a year before his death, Stillman was presented with a gold medal for lifetime service during the second American World Humane Conference in New York City.

In 1938, a new headquarters of the American Humane Association opened on the corner of Dove Street and Washington Avenue in Albany and became known as the Stillman Memorial.

The group phased out its care for children in the 1950s and focused solely on its animal protection and pet anti-cruelty efforts.

The Mohawk Hudson Humane Society remains a not-for-profit organization that has grown steadily since Brad Shear became executive director in 2007.

Today, it has a staff of 35, including one full-time and two part-time veterinarians. It has an annual budget of $2.2 million. More than $126,000

Lori Van Buren / Times Union

Eager dogs at the Mohawk Hudson Humane Society.

was raised in 2014 through the redemption of 1.1 million cans and bottles that people drop off at the facility through its Empties for Animals program. The group's special events, including the Paws in the Park walk and Art Saves Animals fundraiser, raised $246,000 in 2014. It also received about $200,000 in fees from towns and cities and adoption fees.

In 2014, the Mohawk Hudson Humane Society found homes for 3,528 animals and seized more than 270 in animal cruelty investigations.

Among its many services, the group's employees trapped, neutered and returned 58 free-roaming cats and spayed or neutered 449 cats and 324 dogs belonging to low-income owners. More than 141 dogs were trained through obedience classes and 39 therapy dog visits were completed.

The organization leans heavily upon volunteer help; 336 volunteers logged more than 25,000 hours.

"Our mission and focus on

protecting animals has remained consistent across our history," Shear said.

In the past few years, more rescue dogs are being brought up from Southern states and transfers account for 5 percent of the animal intakes. "We've had a very good record in finding homes for the transfer dogs," Shear said. The rest of the dogs and cats are equally divided between local strays and surrenders.

It operates a no-kill shelter.

Bringing a full-time veterinarian on staff starting a decade ago is the most obvious indication of the improved care of animals at the shelter.

"People like adopting dogs here more than ever before," Shear said. "The biggest trend I see is that the popularity of pit bulls keeps rising, and shows no signs of falling off. Pit bulls are great dogs to adopt."

▶ pgrondahl@timesunion.com
▪ 518-454-5623 ▪
@PaulGrondahl

First dogs of Albany, and their mayors

By Paul Grondahl

Mayor Kathy Sheehan let Ozzy, her 11-year-old Boston terrier, put his little paws up on the formidable executive desk in her office at City Hall to pose for a photographer.

The late Mayor Thomas M. Whalen III occasionally allowed his golden retriever, Finn McCool, to romp through the mayor's suite of offices in shaggy exuberance.

Whalen frequently walked around the city with Finn McCool, or down to the Hudson River where the mayor liked to row. He took the dog when he went cross-country skiing at the city's municipal golf course off New Scotland Avenue.

Whalen's faithful dog was cast in bronze and sits beside a statue of the 73rd mayor, who is seated on a park bench in the sculpture. Whalen's right hand rests on the head of his dog. The life-sized monument was installed in 2005 at Tricentennial Park on Broadway, across from the old Union Station downtown. It was designed and created by the late sculptor Hy Rosen, a longtime Times Union editorial cartoonist.

Whalen is the only mayor to have a statue erected in his honor in Albany and McCool is the only dog with that recognition, too. Whalen kept on his desk a clay model of a commissioned statue of his predecessor, Mayor Erastus Corning 2nd, but it was never cast.

Dogs are a recurring theme

Cindy Schultz / Times Union

Mayor Kathy Sheehan and her Boston terrier, Ozzy, in the mayor's office in Albany.

among the mayors of Albany. Corning, who served 11 terms and died in office in 1983, grew up with Irish wolfhounds on his family's grand estate with several hundred acres and a large mansion along Corning Hill Road in Glenmont.

The late state Supreme Court Judge Edward Conway told me when I interviewed him for my biography on Mayor Corning that his father, John Conway, was a longtime friend of political boss Dan O'Connell and O'Connell's personal lawyer. The Conways raised chickens at their house in Troy that O'Connell used for cockfighting — an illegal blood sport that brought the Cornings and O'Connells together and bridged a chasm of class.

O'Connell also raised pit bulls for dog fighting.

"Our dog was killed by a neighbor's German shepherd when I was young and Dan gave us a pit bull from his fighting dogs," Conway recalled. The dog was named Coolidge.

"My dad had to bring Coolidge back to Dan. He said he was sorry we couldn't keep it and he later gave us an Irish setter."

Corning's father, Edwin, introduced Irish wolfhounds to O'Connell, who owned a pair of the huge shaggy dogs that greeted guests at his home off Whitehall Road. He also brought his big dogs, along with a parrot named McGovern, to his summer retreat in the Helderbergs near Thacher Park.

Whalen's successor, five-term Mayor Jerry Jennings, is not a dog owner. "But I remember going to Dan O'Connell's house when I was a kid and having those huge dogs jump on me," Jennings recalled.

It was O'Connell who

uttered a classic line: "All dogs are nicer than most people."

Ozzy came into Sheehan's life as a fifth birthday present for her son, Jay, who is now 15. "He wanted a sibling and for a host of reasons, he ended up with a dog," Sheehan said.

"My dad wouldn't let us have a dog when I was growing up. He said we have six kids, we're not getting a dog," Sheehan said.

Her father's anti-dog position rubbed off on Sheehan, who wrote an essay in high school about over-indulgent dog owners spending more on their pets than their children.

"But you get older and softer," she said. She chose a Boston terrier, in part, because it does not shed much and her husband is allergic to cat hair. She got the 1-year-old dog from a breeder near Syracuse and kept its name as Ozzy because her son liked it.

"Ozzy is great with kids and he's incredibly friendly," Sheehan said. "He's a great companion to my son."

Sheehan took the dog to six weeks of obedience training, "but he wasn't a star pupil," she said. She's glad the training never broke the dog's habit of excitedly jumping up to eye-level with the mayor.

While Sheehan and her husband, Bob, are at work and her son at school, Hounds on the Hudson, an Albany pet care company, takes Ozzy on a walk and to a play group in a dog park each weekday.

Years ago, as a young dog, Ozzy managed to escape

Times Union Archive

"Be Kind To Animal Week" was the occasion for Albany Mayor Erastus Corning 2nd to visit with a pooch and its owner in City Hall. The name of the pup and the young girl are not known.

the Sheehans' yard off New Scotland Avenue near Maria College. They found Ozzy, safe and content, inside the nearby Center for the Disabled, where a staff member fed the stray dog part of a ham sandwich.

Ozzy escaped a few other times and made a beeline to the Center for the Disabled, where he learned to trigger the automatic sliding glass front door. "They liked Ozzy and we always knew where to find him if he ran off," she said. Eventually, they fenced the yard.

One of Ozzy's favorite places is Martha's Vineyard, where the Sheehans have a home.

Her husband, son and Tony, a Chinese exchange student who has lived with the Sheehans for the past three years, take turns walking Ozzy.

The Sheehans have friends who own a Boston terrier named Midge and the two families reciprocate taking care of each other's dogs when traveling.

Sheehan is a dog advocate and is studying whether to add another dog park downtown, off North Pearl Street near Capital Repertory Theatre.

"As long as owners are responsible, dogs are a great asset to the city," she said. "I also get it that we don't want dogs at the Tulip Festival or other city events that draw a lot of people. Overall, I'd say Albany is a dog-friendly city."

Her pet peeve is dog owners who do not pick up after their dog and she wants fines enforced for that infraction.

At 11, Ozzy is long past a habit of jumping up on tables, as he did several years ago where he found a bag of jelly beans, which he ate, without ill effect.

"We're lucky to have Ozzy. He's a great dog," Sheehan said. "I never thought I'd say it, but he's made me a dog person."

▶ *pgrondahl@timesunion. com* ▪ *518-454-5623* ▪ *@PaulGrondahl*

Nipper, Albany's top dog and timeless muse

By Paul Grondahl

A cross the long and rich history of Albany, Nipper ranks as the top dog.

The 28-foot tall, four-ton steel-and-fiberglass canine statue anchored atop a warehouse on North Broadway has captured the hearts and minds of young and old alike for three generations. It's become a landmark and served as a beacon on the city's skyline, visible for miles around downtown and across the Hudson River.

He's been dubbed "the world's largest man-made dog."

Nipper is ingrained in Albany's zeitgeist and has inspired artists and hipsters, fueled Facebook pages and Twitter feeds and created an identity for popular local music and arts website Nippertown.

Nipper has long been the best-selling postcard among the city's iconic images. Nipper is rated the top local attraction on Roadside America, a guide to quirky spaces and places.

The white terrier with black ears and black collar sitting on its haunches with head cocked serves as a sort of North Star.

"As kids, we knew we were almost home whenever we saw Nipper," recalled former Mayor Jerry Jennings, who grew up nearby in North Albany.

"Nipper and the Egg are the two greatest architectural landmarks in Albany. I've always loved Nipper and people come from all over to see it," said musician Greg Haymes, a dog lover and former Times

Lori Van Buren / Times Union

Arnoff Moving and Storage on Broadway is known for its 28-foot fiberglass RCA dog known as Nipper.

Union rock music critic who launched the website Nippertown in 2009.

"I grew up watching Nipper spin around my turntable," said Haymes.

Legendary jazz pianist Lee Shaw, 89, became enamored of Nipper when she arrived in Albany in 1971. She composed a tune, "Nipper's Dream" for the Lee Shaw Trio in 2007.

"I have a tender feeling of nostalgia for that little dog. I tried to capture that feeling musically," she said.

Nipper was a real-life dog in 19th-century England who was painted by the dog owner's brother, Francis Barraud. He depicted the curious dog listening to a gramophone and titled it "His Master's Voice." It became an internationally recognized logo for several

audio recording companies, including RCA.

Nipper became a staple of Americana kitsch, with a vast array of Nipper collectibles.

Nipper came to his downtown Albany perch at 991 Broadway in 1958 following renovations of a rundown reinforced concrete warehouse built in 1900 to house the American Gas Meter Co.

The refurbished structure became the new home of RTA, an appliance distributor specializing in products of RCA.

The owner wanted to make a bold design statement about electronics and hired Albany architect Harris A. Sanders, who came up with the idea of putting RCA's trademark dog atop the building.

The sculpture was fabricated in Chicago, shipped by

rail in five sections, assembled on the roof with the help of a 10-story crane, and attached to a metal frame.

Nipper statues became popular roadside attractions across the Northeast, but many were removed or the dogs became homeless after the buildings where they were perched were torn down.

When RCA sales declined in Albany, the Broadway warehouse distributed Sanyo and other electronic and appliance brands until it closed. The building was used as a furniture store, flea market and art gallery and Nipper's steady gaze remained high overhead during all its iterations.

Nipper's right ear was pierced with what looks like an earring from afar, but is actually an aircraft beacon to alert low-flying airplanes.

Alejandro del Peral, 28, of Albany opened Nine Pin Ciderworks at 929 Broadway in February 2014, thrilled to be starting a business in the shadow of Nipper. "We love Nipper because we can see him from everywhere," he said.

He adopted a Lab/terrier mix from a dog rescue organization in Chatham, Columbia County, as Nine Pin's mascot, Samba the Cider Dog.

"Samba only weighs about 20 pounds and has shorter front legs, so when he sits down he has that perfect Nipper pose," del Peral said. "Our customers started noticing."

Nine Pin's graphic designer and photographer, Joe Klockowski, got a forklift and lifted Samba onto Nine Pine's

Times Union archive
Nipper stands guard in Albany.

roof. The dog sat in the Nipper pose, Klockowski captured the image and the Samba-Nipper doppelganger effect now graces the company's website.

Nipper continues to resonate across the region. An Instagram and Twitter feed, DogCalledNipper, has more than 300 followers for its inventive posts and tweets that Photoshop the iconic dog and gramophone into various pop-culture images.

Nippertown founder Haymes understands the strange attraction. "He's the great sentinel of Albany. First of all, he's a dog and people who love dogs really looooove dogs," Haymes said. "Also, you don't see giant dogs on top of buildings that often."

Haymes recalled that Charlene Shortsleeve, who owned the popular punk club QE2, used Nipper on her club's Central Avenue sign and its calendars and posters. There's also a Nipper photo or work of art at the Mohawk Hudson Humane Society's annual Art Saves Animals art auction and reception fundraiser. Haymes and his wife, Sara Ayers, served on the honorary committee.

The couple's Australian

cattle dogs Cale (who died at 17 in September) and Shelby, 7, are listed as Nippertown's advisory board below a picture of the dogs.

Alas, Nipper's current owner, Arnoff Moving and Storage, has put the warehouse up for sale. The company bought the building in 1997 from RTA Corp. Over the years, Mike Arnoff, company president, paid for two major Nipper rehabs. He also had the fiberglass skin power washed and painted.

Arnoff will urge any prospective buyer to preserve Nipper, although the statue's long-term future is uncertain. "We've had a lot of activity and several offers, but we haven't accepted one yet," Arnoff said in late April. "Several developers seem very serious about keeping Nipper on the building as a landmark."

Nipper has no formal legal protection as a landmark, although its place in the heart and soul of the city is unassailable.

"I think I speak for everyone in the city when I say Nipper should stay," said Mayor Kathy Sheehan, owner of a Boston terrier named Ozzy. "He's a landmark seated on the right building, right where he belongs."

"It will be hard to say goodbye," Arnoff said, "but I'm willing to take Nipper with me if need be in order to save him," he said.

▶ pgrondahl@timesunion. com ▪ 518-454-5623 ▪ @PaulGrondahl

Owney the postal dog's epic story, his own stamp

By Paul Grondahl

No other dog in Albany history has a legend that transcends the fame of Owney, the plucky orphaned Irish terrier mix who was the city's beloved 19th-century postal mascot.

Immortalized in books, films, souvenir merchandise and the National Postal Museum in Washington, D.C., the dog's visage appeared on a 44-cent forever stamp and commemorative postmark that was part of an official Owney Day in Albany in 2011.

The Owney saga began in 1888 after the stray mutt curled up on a pile of mailbags and fell asleep.

Postal workers adopted the orphaned mongrel and let the dog ride atop mail in horse-drawn wagons from the post office two blocks to Union Station on Broadway.

Soon, his horizons expanded as Owney was allowed to ride mail trains. Before turning him loose, Albany postal clerks bought him a collar with a return address: "Owney, Post Office, Albany, New York."

The genesis of the dog's name is uncertain. It might have been a variation of an Albany mail carrier named Owens, who gave the dog special attention. Or, Owney may have grown out of initial questioning at the post office: "Who's your owner?" and "Who owns you?"

The "tramp mail dog" was

Times Union archive photos

Owney was the unofficial mascot of the Railway Mail Service. Below, Owney's U.S. Postal Service Forever stamp.

the subject of scores of 1890s newspaper articles. One claimed the scrawny mutt stood guard over a mail sack that had fallen from a wagon to protect its contents from thieves.

The popular pooch made a guest appearance at the 1892 Republican National Convention in Buffalo and a crowd of 300 turned out to meet him during a 1896 visit to Brattleboro, Vt.

Postal workers considered Owney a good luck charm in an era when the job was a dangerous one due to train derailments, explosions and robberies. The trains the dog rode on managed to reach

their destinations unscathed. Workers began attaching leather and metal baggage tags to Owney's collar to mark his travels. The shiny tokens became so numerous and heavy that in 1894 Postmaster General John Wanamaker presented Owney with a harness-like jacket that more evenly distributed the weight of his fame. The dog eventually logged more than 140,000 miles on the rails.

In 1895, Owney was sent on an around-the-world sailing voyage as a goodwill ambassador. He traveled with a dog-size suitcase holding a blanket, his comb and a brush. He was shipped under a special mail classification: "Registered Dog Package."

By early 1897, Owney was old and failing. He had gone blind in one eye, could only chew soft food and turned ornery in retirement when he was confined to the Albany post office. In June of that

Owney, U.S. Railway Mail Service mascot, poses in a mail train with some of his friends. Below, Owney sits with an identified Albany postal worker.

year, Owney stowed away on a mail train bound for Toledo, Ohio. During an interview with a Toledo newspaper reporter, the terrier lashed out and bit a postal worker. On June 11, 1897, Owney was shot and killed, probably by a U.S. marshal, although nobody claimed responsibility for the deed.

Postal clerks took up a collection and had Owney stuffed. The taxidermy was displayed at the Post Office Department's headquarters in Washington, D.C. In 1911, it was donated to the Smithsonian Institution's National Postal Museum, where Owney

remains a popular attraction.

The dog's tale is published in children's books, including "A Lucky Dog," (2003) written by Dirk Wales and illustrated

by Diane Kenna.

▶ *This article was taken from two stories that first appeared in the Times Union.*

Bailey saves the day

By Michele Delehanty

Bailey was a yellow Lab who belonged to my son Bryan and his wife, Natasha.

He was just a puppy when he came into our lives. He was a typical Lab — lovable, nutty and stubborn. We often said that when God was passing out brains, Bailey was behind the door.

Nothing bothered him. When Bryan and Natasha had twins, Megan and Bryan Jr., the dog took it in stride and became their best friend.

Bailey was happiest when he was in the midst of the family. His worth became evident one summer day when the twins were about 2 years old. Megan was sleeping on the sofa and Bryan Jr. needed attention. Natasha left Megan and took Bryan into their room. She was only out of sight for a few minutes, but when she came back, Megan was gone and so was Bailey.

Somehow, Megan had opened the back door and gone out. They did not have a fenced-in yard and there were woods all around. Natasha panicked and went out the door yelling for Meg and Bailey. They couldn't have gotten too far; it was only a minute or two. Realizing they were gone, she called the police.

The community where they lived did not have its own police department so the area was covered by the New

Photo provided by Michele Delehanty

Bailey, the yellow Lab.

York State Police. Within minutes, several troop cars were at the house. They questioned Natasha. When the troopers found out Bailey was gone, too, they were concerned that the dog might be a problem. She assured the troopers he was not a vicious dog and would cause the police no harm.

The troopers began looking through the woods. There were so many places a small child could have fallen. It took about half an hour to find Megan.

An Amber Alert was just about to be issued and helicopters dispatched when a trooper found Megan and Bailey together under a tree. He had never left her side.

The trooper asked the little

girl if she was Megan and she said she was and that Bailey had gotten lost. There was no fear: She had her loyal companion with her and no harm could come to her.

Bailey greeted the trooper with his usual kindness and gleefully followed him home.

Needless to say, Bailey was a hero in our book. We often tell the kids the story. They never tire of hearing it.

Many years later, the infirmities of old age became too much for him and the family made a difficult decision.

A new Lab has come into their house, not to replace Bailey, but to create new memories.

▶ *Contributor Michele Delehanty lives in Colonie.*

Police K-9 Memorial recalls heroic dogs

By Paul Grondahl

When Albany police patrolman Douglas Nadoraski and his police K-9 Ed arrived on the scene at Lexington Avenue, a man was slashing with a large butcher knife at three officers who tried to subdue him.

Nadoraski gave the command to his specially trained German shepherd, who charged the assailant and pinned him to the ground.

"Ed did not ask questions. He leaped into action," Nadoraski, of Albany, recalled of the incident that occurred several years ago. As two injured police officers were taken to a hospital for treatment, Nadoraski took Ed to a veterinarian, who stitched up the dog's knife cuts.

"I always knew I could count on Ed," he said. "My dogs became an extension of myself. They were my partners and my best friends. They always did what I told them to do and never complained."

In addition to his own, Nadoraski trained three dozen other police dogs in his career.

His voice became choked with emotion as he stood at the grave markers of his three police dogs: Ed (1986-96), Guy (1992-2001) and Stevens "Stevie" (2000-08).

The German shepherds are buried at the Police K-9 Memorial at the Mohawk Hudson Humane Society in Menands.

Nadoraski, who retired in

Lori Van Buren / Times Union

Police K-9 trainer Douglas Nadoraski stands next to the memorial at the Mohawk Hudson Humane Society in Menands.

2009 after 36 years as a patrolman and K-9 trainer for the Albany Police Department, was a driving force in creating the memorial and police dog cemetery in 1999.

"Our dogs are a big part of our lives, even when they retire," he said of the dogs that live at home with the handlers. The remains of more than 50 police dogs are buried at the site, marked by gray granite markers with their names, departments, badge numbers and years of K-9 service.

The memorial features a large granite monument with a German shepherd police dog sculpture on top.

K-9 police officers, family and friends gather for a memorial ceremony each May.

Nadoraski said it is hard to articulate the special bond.

He recalled his K-9 Guy sniffing out bomb-making supplies in a house near Lin-

coln Park and locating explosives on other occasions. His dogs Stevie and Guy located elderly people suffering from Alzheimer's disease who were wandering in the woods.

Once, Nadoraski sent Ed after a suspect fleeing a burglary. "Ed caught the burglar, but the dog and the burglar both got sprayed by a skunk," he said.

Nadoraski praised the efforts of Jim Teller, a retired Albany K-9 officer, and his wife, Kate, who volunteer to maintain the memorial site.

"It's a good feeling knowing our dogs are in a peaceful, beautiful setting," he said.

Nadoraski does not have a dog anymore. "I don't know if my heart would take it anymore. There's only so much room in my heart," he said.

▶ *pgrondahl@timesunion. com* ▪ *518-454-5623* ▪ *@PaulGrondahl*

The Railroad Puppy becomes a therapy dog

Richard Nash with Hudson, the railroad puppy, at the Capitol in Albany.

By Richard Nash

Hudson and two siblings were just 3 weeks old when they were found nailed to the railroad tracks in Albany.

Hudson's paw was cut off. Sadly, one dog, Carina, did not make it, but after lifesaving treatment, Hudson and his sister Pearl became known as the Railroad Puppies.

Veterinarians decided Hudson was a great candidate for a prosthetic limb. He was one of the first dogs in the state to be fitted with an artificial paw.

His life was changed when he was rescued. Our life changed when he adopted us. He lives with two rescued dogs (a pit bull mix and a Pomeranian mix) and eight rescued cats that all get along. It's all about how you raise them and the love you have to share.

After Hudson adopted us, I knew he was special and could do great things and spread awareness about animal cruelty. I got him into training with the goal that we would become a therapy dog team. We did it.

Now we visit schools, hospitals and adult day care facilities. We are also hospice volunteers, visiting with patients and their families. We try to teach everyone we meet that just because you're different, you are still special in your own "wooftastic" way.

Hudson brings smiles to everyone he meets. I believe in my heart that Hudson was put on this Earth to not only show that anyone can overcome adversity but for the love and joy he brings to others.

Hudson the Railroad Puppy is changing hearts and minds about the pit bull-type breeds one woof at a time.

Our motto is "Caring & Sharing & Pawing it Forward."

Hudson has a lot of love to share with the world now that he has been given the chance.

▶ *Contributor Richard Nash lives in Schodack.*

Scamp had a particular love for babies

By Lois Pasternack

Our dog Scamp was a poodle-schnauzer or schnoodle mix we brought home when he was just 9 weeks old.

He loved everyone and assumed everyone loved him back, which they usually did.

Scamp was a highly intelligent, sensitive dog, much more interested in the people around him than in other dogs. He enjoyed being around people so much that after about a year my husband, Dr. Jonathan Pasternack, began to take him to work at his pediatric practice in Delmar several days a week.

Scamp was soon a celebrity for Jonathan's patients and their parents. He especially loved babies.

Once we retired, we spent the winter months in our home in Tucson, Ariz. As a rule, Scamp preferred to be in the shade, so it got my attention one day when he remained on the river rocks in full sun, intent on something.

Suddenly, he walked over to Jonathan, sat on his haunches and looked up at Jon, with his mouth partially open. Jon patted him on the head and went back to his conversation. But Scamp held his pose and touched Jon's knee with one paw.

Scamp gently placed what looked like a bit of dark rock at Jon's feet. It felt nothing like stone when I picked it up.

I turned the object over

Photo courtesy of Lois Pasternack

Scamp meets children at Dr. Jonathan Pasternack's Delmar office.

with my finger and saw a speck of yellow ... was that a closed eye? I realized it was a baby bird.

Scamp had plucked a baby hummingbird off of the hot river rocks, and he knew it needed help. It was nearly dead from dehydration.

I lined a container with a dish towel and put the limp hatchling inside of it. Scamp stayed right in the kitchen next to the table where the bird was, whining anxiously.

I used a toothpick to trickle a few drops of water onto the tip of its beak. And again. Several minutes passed without success. I had nearly conceded failure when the long, curved filament that is a humming-

bird's tongue — finer than sewing thread — flickered out of its beak and caught one of the water drops.

We took Scamp's bird to a wildlife rescue and rehabilitation center. They assured us the bird would be fine.

It came to me later that Scamp's anxiety had disappeared when we arrived at the center. It is as if he recognized that we had come to a place where his foundling would be in good hands. He slept in the backseat all the way home, satisfied he had made a difference in the life of a baby.

▶ *Contributor Lois Pasternack splits her time between Slingerlands and Tucson, Ariz.*

Peyton the hero saved multiple lives

By Lucy Warren

On Sept. 15, 2011, my golden retriever, Peyton, saved my life from carbon monoxide poisoning.

I came home from work and the house was a little chilly so I put the heat on for the first time that year. My husband was driving home from work and was about four hours away. Around 7:15 p.m. or so I became very tired. It did not dawn on me that something was wrong since I have diabetes and get tired at times. I couldn't keep my eyes open so I decided to lie down on the couch for a while.

Around 8:30 p.m., Peyton jumped on my chest and kept barking. He was jumping on me so hard that it felt like he was going through my body.

As I was waking, I tried to yell at him to get down, but I had no voice. I couldn't breathe and I was choking. The fumes were horrible and I was dizzy and out of it. I called 911 and took Peyton and my other dog, Roxy, outside with me.

When the fire department arrived, my carbon monoxide level was at 325 ppm. They called in the gas company and told me if I had slept for another 20 minutes my husband would have come home to a dead wife and two dead dogs.

The fire department did a great job cleaning up my house and the furnace man fixed the broken exhaust pipe.

Peyton was recognized as a hero. Each fireman shook his paw and he received a Hero Certificate from the fire department.

I am so grateful that I am here to tell his story. He never leaves my side, always making sure that I am OK. He will forever be my hero.

▶ *Contributor Lucy Warren lives in Niskayuna.*

Photo courtesy of Lucy Warren

Peyton with a firefighter hat.

A rainbow of Labs brightens workplace

By Bill Deegan

One of the benefits of my job is that I get to bring my dog to work.

Patches is a 7-year-old chocolate Lab. At work, Patches enjoys the company of Bruce, a 2-year-old yellow Lab, and Eli, a 6-month-old black Lab.

Patches is low-key and kind of shy while Bruce is a little high strung and a big chicken. Eli is working on his personality. All three get along and all are proficient at making friends, especially if food is involved. It is pretty hard to resist three sets of big brown eyes staring at you and three dogs drooling at the same time.

These guys are not watchdogs because they can be bribed with a dog treat or piece of doughnut. Nor are they fierce protectors, preferring to be adored, petted and given treats or to chew cardboard.

Most dogs are creatures of habit and have incredible internal clocks. These dogs know when the doughnuts come and park themselves by the counter to wait. If the doughnuts are late, the pacing and whimpering begins.

When the doughnuts arrive, they go into the boss' office where he divides up the goodies. The dogs often have jelly or powdered sugar on their faces and heads.

Their other major daily appointment is their evening walk. After work, I take Patch-

Photo courtesy of Bill Deegan

Bruce, left, Eli and Patches eagerly await their noontime snack.

es and Bruce for a walk on the property (Eli is too young).

Around 4 p.m., Patches will lie under my desk and Bruce behind my chair. They watch any movement I make, in anticipation of our walk.

When we go for our walk, I do not need a leash since it is private property, mostly farmland, and the dogs can roam freely but they stay close.

It does not matter if it's 5 below or 95 degrees, snowing, sleeting or raining. The walk must happen. The intensity of their looks, the pacing and weird noises they make in anticipation makes it impossible for me to deny their trip.

We have encountered many animals, mostly deer, rabbits, woodchucks, ducks and geese and even a coyote. The Labs often give chase but it is mostly

for show because they have not yet caught anything.

Their favorite activities are jumping in water or mud and chasing and chewing sticks. They love a nice piece of maple or oak and to have a tug of war.

Few things are more enjoyable than being with these dogs on a walk, watching their tails wagging in anticipation and their intensity in their playing and chasing each other.

It is therapeutic for them and me, especially after a hard day. These guys can make a gray sky blue. I cannot imagine not liking a dog, the love and attention they give for really not much in return and knowing they will always be there for you and you for them.

▶ *Contributor Bill Deegan lives in Troy.*

Astro is happy to be alive

By Dan Lundquist

Astro arrived at night.

We had been living on the farm for about six months, and a big house, two barns and 11 acres along the Upper Hudson River was feeling like a lot for the two of us and our golden retriever, Sammy.

Sammy seemed very happy to roam the property without a hint of loneliness. She tended to stay close to the house or barn and, when she did wander, would come after a loud whistle.

Beth sent me a link to the Web page for Eleventh Hour, so named because the clock is ticking on its residents. The featured dog was a cute-looking black Lab named Astro – a sweet and energetic 4-year-old with a limp who hails from Alabama.

We agreed to a home visit with the Skidmore student who was fostering him and an EHR volunteer.

Sammy is a sweet and gentle typical golden. Astro was, well, what? He was something besides or in addition to black Lab, maybe part pit bull?

The dogs lollygagged back and forth between the house and barn before we brought them inside. They explored it at high speed before they eventually calmed down and joined us.

"They are like 'black and tan,'" the Skidmore student said. We decided on a trial run.

Photo courtesy of Dan Lundquist

Astro, aka Sky, a rescue dog.

The intervening weeks were smooth and natural. Sammy and Astro had almost no acclimation problems. And Astro seemed to have no traumas at all. He just seemed ... happy.

Happy to play in the snow, a first for a Southern boy. He has learned better, but it was really funny to watch him get up a head of speed running — sprinting — from a far field toward the barn only to hit the slick, packed snow in the drive and keep going until he hit a drift or a barn door or me.

Astro's name didn't seem to fit. So, from Astro came the sky, and from the sky came Schuyler from the nearby town of Schuylerville. Off we went to PetSmart to get the tag engraved, and a collar, dog bed, toys and chews.

He's gentle. He's fast. He's strong and deferential. He has become well-mannered, though it took dog-proofing the bed and other furniture. He is beginning to relax more, but still stares at me with his opaque black-on-black visage. He still doesn't obey voice commands. He hasn't gotten up on the stove like he did in the early days, but he still, every meal, starts eating his food as it pours out of the container into his bowl. And he still is, always will be, a very messy drinker.

▶ *Contributor Dan Lundquist lives in Saratoga Springs.*

Foster dogs leave a piece of themselves

**By Sean Manning
and Tracy Bailey**

This story isn't just about our 7-year-old dog, Logan, it is about our other 15 dogs and counting who have been rescued, fostered and adopted to loving homes. It could be the plot of a television show.

The journey began with Thad, Marley, Jack, Roscoe, Corky, Roscoe 2.0 (Tracy's favorite), Ray, Sonya, Ollie, Mama, Sky, Finn, Lilly, Buster, Walker, Roscoe 2.0 again (we almost adopted him) and last, but certainly not least, our beloved yellow Lab, Logan, who we have had since he was only a few months old.

We cannot tell you how much we love fostering dogs and the fulfillment these dogs bring to our lives. Each and every dog has a story to tell and we take pride in believing that the time these dogs are in our care has been the best weeks or months of their lives.

We could go on and on about specific stories but we wanted to tell a larger story about saving lives when there is no financial obligation, and the only requirement is time, effort and some patience. The first question we always get is, "How do you not adopt them? I would fall in love with every one and keep them."

They are right, it is not easy

Photo courtesy of Sean Manning and Tracy Bailey
Lilly the foster dog with Logan.

having a foster dog be adopted, but knowing they are going to a great forever home with great people makes the transition to the next dog much easier.

There are many more dogs out there who need a home, not a cage, and we are constantly surprised by how good these surrendered or stray dogs are after just a few weeks of structure and a brother like Logan.

Logan is a patient, playful and loving dog. If it weren't

for his welcoming personality, it would be nearly impossible for us to bring in all these brothers and sisters for him.

We'd like to conclude this story by thanking Homeward Bound Dog Rescue for all they do. This is a cause we believe so much in. They create awareness for these animals we care so much about.

▶ *Contributors Sean Manning and Tracy Bailey live in Glenmont.*

The pointer sisters

By Renee Pizzo-Roy

I was first introduced to Maggie when I started dating my now-husband, Tony. At the time, she was about 1½ years old. Tony's home consisted of two dogs (Katie and Maggie) and two cats.

As I entered his house, I was greeted by an energetic dog with a toy in her mouth. Her stub of a tail ferociously wagged, accompanied with a butt shake to match the fierce rhythm. The expression on her face was like this was the best moment of her life.

I was a little taken aback by her excitement but there was something about her that made me want to play with her.

As Tony and I continued to date, I realized that if I was going to be a part of this pack, I needed to know my place — which was second to Maggie. Thus began a friendly rivalry. Maggie slept next to Tony and tolerated nothing else. She had many tactics to keep me in my place in the bed.

First was the quick crawl. Starting at our feet, she would squirm between us until she reached our heads, using her body weight to push me over.

Second was walking over and on me until she was comfortably situated next to Tony.

Lastly was the I'm-going-to-sit-on-your-head-'til-you-move tactic. It was like I was invisible and not even in the bed.

I also learned that I needed to protect my food.

I had a tendency to sit on the edge of my seat when I ate, my fork in one hand and the other

Photo courtesy of Renee Pizzo-Roy

Daisy, Maggie and Katie, the German shorthaired pointers.

protecting my plate from Katie. Maggie would climb onto the chair behind me and rest her head on my shoulder.

She would allow me a couple of forkfuls and then dive her head over my shoulder to obtain her portion.

One year, Katie died around the time we went on our annual vacation at Indian Lake. We stayed inside by the fire and grieved Katie's passing. I started to see Maggie differently. She was not the most well-behaved dog but she was funny, loving and devoted. The realization that a dog's life is not forever and that they could leave us at any moment reminded me to appreciate Maggie more.

I remember saying to Tony, "Why don't we get another German shorthaired pointer?" We got our second pointer and then our third.

Maggie, too, started to show

signs that I met her approval. I would get less frustrated with her. I would snuggle more with her in bed, laugh at her behavior and accept her for the way she was. In turn, she accepted that I was part of the family.

In December 2014, an X-ray revealed that Maggie had cancer at the age of 13. She lived about three weeks after being diagnosed. We spent as much time with her as we could and did all her favorite activities.

Maggie peacefully left this Earth in her favorite position, lying between us, but most of all being held by Tony. There's a hole in our hearts that I don't think will ever be filled but I'm learning to live with sleeping directly next to my husband and eating without the immediate threat of having my food taken away from me.

▶ Contributor Renee Pizzo-Roy lives in North Greenbush.

Micah rides the bus

By Sue Raynis

It was a sunny, breezy morning in May, and I had just let the dogs — five Labrador retrievers — out into the fenced backyard after their breakfast.

I was puttering around upstairs when I heard a loud knocking on my door. I looked outside to see a man I didn't know, a CDTA STAR bus parked in the street, and to my horror, two of my dogs with the man, very pleased to be meeting a new BFF. He said he saw five dogs wander out of the garage and head toward the street and knew something was wrong.

The door to the backyard had blown open and I had forgotten to close the overhead garage door when I had taken out the trash that morning.

I thanked the driver, bribed the two dogs who had stayed with him with the always-reliable "cookie!" and put them inside. Without really thinking, I grabbed a couple of leashes and ran across the street into the adjacent neighborhood. The driver proceeded to his stop next door.

Belle, the leader of the pack, had taken her two buddies on a wild run and they were circling back as I screamed their names, so I had them with me fairly quickly. The problem was that I was on the side street facing my house and had to get back across my busy street.

Photo courtesy of Sue Raynis

Micah, the yellow Lab.

I had three dogs and only two leashes and the dogs were really hyped up from the run. So now I was stuck with only Belle and Sophie on leashes. I knew Micah would stay with us, but worried that once we started for home, he would make a break for the house and get hit crossing the street.

While I was trying to figure out a creative way to make the math of three dogs and two leashes work, the CDTA bus pulled out of my neighbor's driveway, turned onto the side street and pulled up next to me. Opening the door, the driver said, "If you put him on the bus, I can take him across the street for you."

Micah did not think climbing onto a large strange vehicle was a good idea, but with my neighbors and the driver coaxing, he cautiously climbed the steps onto the bus. Once on board, he did a happy meet-and-greet, then settled right down. I walked the girls safely across the street.

The bus driver did a U-turn, crossed the street, pulled into my driveway, opened the door, and Micah hopped off the bus like he'd been riding all his life. Day saved! Thank you, CDTA driver, whoever you are!

▶ *Contributor Sue Raynis lives in Colonie.*

The darling No. 1 pup of The Palazzo Riggi

Photo courtesy of Michele Riggi

Michele Riggi plants a kiss on the cheek of her beloved Chihuahua, Kahlua.

By Michele Riggi

The most important part of The Palazzo Riggi is the 41 Posh Palazzo Pups and our beautiful cat, Emerald. They all are very special, but I am going to tell you about how this all began. The start of what I call the "Chihuahua Revolution" began with my sweet little Kahlua. He was that little "Doggie in the Window" when he found me almost 18 years ago. His precious disposition was adorable in every way; he was smart and would sing a song for his adoring audience with the slightest command. He always welcomed everyone with a kiss and a wagging tail.

As the pack at The Palazzo Riggi grew over the years, Kahlua welcomed every brother and sister with a polite sniff and an acceptance as any gallant pack leader would do. Never once over the years did he ever not accept a sibling. Kahlua's life was as fabulous as his personality. He never gave up even when he became blind and deaf. His sense of smell never failed him. He would find his way to me wherever I was, just to give me his love. Until his last breath we were together and loved each other more than ever. Kahlua will always be my first and my favorite. I miss him with all my heart and know he is running and playing with his siblings over the rainbow bridge. Bless you, my loving Kahlua.

▶ *Contributor Michele Riggi lives in Saratoga Springs.*

Country and city dogs in one small house

By Cindy Schultz

Photo courtesy of Cindy Schultz
Dogs from left are Rosie, Oliver, Peanut and Hap.

Four dogs in my little Albany house? The notion never crossed my mind until my friend Jane asked me to pet sit her cute little Chihuahua. She couldn't take Peanut with her while she wintered in Florida. Oh, and by the way, did I mind taking her schnauzer, Hap, too? In return, Jane offered to give my husband and me a week in her timeshare anywhere in the country.

I said I'd ask Jason, thinking he'd say "no" for sure. We had Rosie, a beagle-pit bull mix, and Oliver, a rat terrier. To my surprise, he said "yes."

Really? I'm the animal lover, and Jason's more the animal tolerator.

I told Jane we'd take both pets. She dropped them off, along with their sweaters, jackets, leashes, crates, blankets, bowls, food, treats, pills and distilled water. She explained that her dogs have special needs. Peanut has a bad ticker and could go into cardiac arrest and die at any moment. Hap had to take daily potassium pills and drink distilled water or he might develop kidney stones. Also, he should be brushed daily or his coat gets gnarled and nasty. And did I know how to express their anal glands? I smiled and suggested a second week at the timeshare would sure be nice. Jane quickly dropped the topic.

Six-pound Peanut established her dominance straightaway when she nipped Rosie's ear and growled at Oliver. And we learned Hap despised playtime. He'd snatch toys away from our dogs and stockpile them in his crate.

The usually easy task of dog walking suddenly became a big undertaking. We figured out a system that mostly worked. I picked up a leash coupler to fasten the two big dogs together and the small ones walked on separate leashes. Even so, the dogs would go every which way and someone got tangled up, usually me. If another dog walked past, they all lunged and jumped and barked.

Jason stayed firm on his "no dogs in the bed" rule so everyone slept in their respective crates at night. An early riser, Jason would let the dogs out in the morning and feed them breakfast. Once he left for work, Peanut would crawl under the covers with me.

When I woke up, all I'd see was the front half of her body under the covers, hind legs sprawled out on a pillow and tail wagging. She was way too cute to reprimand.

Many times it was total mayhem. Our dogs were used to city sounds, but Peanut and Hap were country bumpkins. Urban life for them was new and exciting. People and dogs walked past the house, delivery trucks rumbled down the road, airplanes flew overhead and letter carriers infiltrated the porch. One dog would start barking, and the whole lot joined in for a massive bark fest. I could usually tune them out, but Jason would go absolutely bonkers. But he could silence them all in a snap when he put his foot down and bellowed, "Enough!"

▶ *Contributor Cindy Schultz lives in Albany and works at the Times Union.*

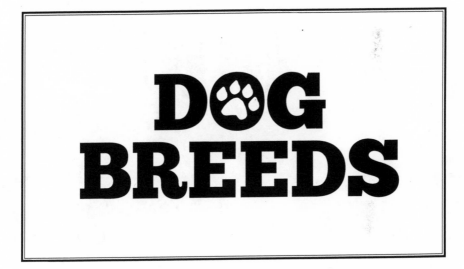

Gizmo helped counselor learn to reflect

By Kathleen Bracken

I grew up with dogs – German shepherds, actually. For most of my childhood, there was a dog in my house. I love animals, and am definitely a dog person.

In elementary school, I imagined being grown up with a dog of my own. I would check out one book in the Scotland Elementary School library over and over – it detailed all the dog breeds.

A few months after my University at Albany graduation, finally on my own, I decided it was time for a dog. My research began. I read books and looked online to re-familiarize myself with the different breeds. All of them seemed amazing.

I felt like I was unable to narrow things down, so I asked a few friends. Unfailingly, they told me that whatever dog they had was the best.

That's when I realized that, at some point, I needed to take a step back from all the information and recommendations, and think about myself. I lived in a one-bedroom apartment with my beloved guinea pig. This disqualified many dogs.

And, if I was being honest, while I enjoyed picturing myself running on hiking trails with a canine companion, in my actual life I needed a dog that would enjoy watching four hours of "Beverly Hills, 90210" on the couch.

Ultimately, I chose a Shih

Photo courtesy of Kathleen Bracken
Kathleen Bracken with Gizmo, a Shih-Tzu.

Tzu. You can imagine the horror on my parents' faces when I brought a tiny ball of fluff into the home of German shepherd lovers. But Gizmo makes me feel like I won the dog lottery.

Is he perfect? No. He needs expensive grooming, and he eats leaves and vomits them on the bath mats. But he makes me happy every day. He is 13.

Now I work as the college counselor at the Doane Stuart School. In conversations with students about college and choice, I often think of Gizmo.

When faced with countless opportunities, it's easy to start gathering information. It's reasonable to ask others for their opinions. But equally important in major decisions is the ability to do some self-reflection. That's a really important part of thinking about college, and life. My younger self surely wouldn't have predicted my career or Gizmo. But they are integral parts of my identity.

▶ *Contributor Kathleen Bracken lives in Latham.*

Daisy loved water and a game of catch

By Nelson Carpenter

I remember having lunch with my wife and two children at Salty's Pub in Clifton Park debating what to name our new Lab puppy.

This was an important discussion since this puppy would attempt to take the place of our recently departed Coco, a wonderful mutt who had been with our son and daughter since birth.

We decided on the name Daisy feeling that, if it was good enough for Dagwood and Blondie, it was perfect for us.

Daisy was a typical Lab who loved the water in almost any form, from ponds and lakes to stagnant muddy puddles. For whatever reason, our hikes in local state parks always seemed to end with a quick jump into some smelly pile of dirt or a muddy hole.

But, like most dogs, the one type of water Daisy didn't care for was bath water. Yet we always managed to clean the car, and Daisy, once we got home.

She occasionally snuck down the street to the neighborhood community pool for a quick swim. After several forays, someone called the neighborhood association president to complain. Since I was the president, I gave Daisy and myself a stern lecture and waited until her next break-in.

She was athletic and adept at retrieving sticks. She really loved catching balls, so much so that it often became dif-

Photo courtesy of Nelson Carpenter

Daisy the dog, bikes and a station wagon signal summer vacation for the Carpenter family.

ficult to practice catch in the backyard with my daughter, Maureen, and son, Michael, both playing ball with school teams. If Daisy saw us practicing, she would sneak up and begin intercepting thrown softballs and baseballs, quickly turning our "practice" sessions into Daisy playtime. Once, her "sneak up" was actually a dive through the porch screen door, wrecking the screen, yet getting to the ball on the ground first since all of our eyes were on her hustle.

Daisy loved to "work" every morning in the mid-1990s, helping Maureen deliver the Times Union. On recommendations from her customers,

Maureen was named carrier of the month. The accompanying write-up in the TU focused on Daisy, who went from house to house to assure the paper was delivered properly. Once Daisy heard the paper fall, she scampered off to the next house.

Once the kids left for college, Daisy became my wife Maryellen's constant companion and insistent follower, never leaving her alone. Maryellen occasionally protested, but since I traveled a lot on my job, I knew that she appreciated the company.

▶ *Contributor Nelson Carpenter lives in Saratoga Springs.*

Duke the Dalmatian brought people together

By Eileen A. Clinton

The details may be a bit fuzzy but the emotions are still very real.

It was about 1967 when I first met Duke, a beautiful Dalmatian. I had never seen a spotted dog like him before except on TV. Duke was accompanied by an elderly scruffy man, Mr. Gray.

The man and dog were walking around Washington Park directly across from my home when I first caught sight of them. Without hesitation, I crossed over to meet the uniquely spotted dog. I asked permission to pet Duke and his owner quickly approved my request. I bent over and smothered the four-legged creature with tons of attention.

It was love at first sight.

Duke and I made an immediate connection as his owner looked on with pleasure. A few minutes passed and Mr. Gray invited me to accompany him and Duke for a walk around the park. Of course, I accepted without thinking twice.

Within a short amount of time I knew all about Duke and his fascinating background. He was a movie star. Remember "101 Dalmatians"? Duke was one of the Dalmatians in the movie. Mr. Gray was delighted to share his special story with me and explain how dog met man as well as Duke's Hollywood stardom. I was all ears as he told me that his doctor, Lawrence Porcelli, was responsible for getting Duke

Photo courtesy of Eileen A. Clinton

Duke the Dalmatian, became Eileen Clinton's dog.

for him. When Mr. Gray was hospitalized, Dr. Porcelli told him he needed more exercise and had to get outdoors more often. The perfect solution was Duke, who Dr. Porcelli just happened to find for Mr. Gray. Duke was exactly what the doctor ordered and helped Mr. Gray improve his health. The entire story was fascinating but honestly, I was just a little girl who fell in love with a dog.

When I returned home that day, I told my mother about my new friends and she was furious. What was I thinking talking to a total stranger? I was insistent that there was nothing to worry about and

told her all about Duke, my new pal. The next day, my mom demanded to meet Mr. Gray before she would allow me to see Duke again. Mr. Gray won her over and that was the beginning of a wonderful relationship between our families.

Duke remained my buddy and Mr. Gray was like an uncle to me until his death. They were both very special to me.

Duke was a lifesaver and dear companion to an aging man in poor health. Mr. Gray died at the age of 84 and Duke was left to me in his will.

▶ *Contributor Eileen A. Clinton lives in Troy.*

Photographing dogs in the course of play

Photo courtesy of Michael Kalin

Toby and Emily, from the Labrador retriever page on AlbanyDogs.net

By Julie Elson

One might assume, based on weather and availability of light, that a golf course in the Northeast would have its greatest usage from April into November, but that is not the case with Albany's municipal golf course, Capital Hills at Albany.

For many, when the golfers leave, dog-walking season begins. People park their cars, dog faces eagerly steaming the windows, everything ready, doors open and off they go. Humans dutifully follow.

The dogs relish the opportunity to walk on- or off-leash along the well-maintained path, but nothing beats running free across the greens, with an occasional quick dip in the Normans Kill. Some bark and chase balls, others proudly carry sticks, some have coats of many colors, some with muzzles of gray totter happily through nine holes while others run all 18, most falling asleep on the way home.

Photographing these four-legged visitors has become the winter work and pleasure of my husband, Michael Kalin.

Growing up, Michael never had a pet, though he has fond memories of the times his family baby-sat Rosebud, a neighbor's bulldog.

Michael discovered dogs in a roundabout way through his interest in photography.

After he retired, he took up kayaking, and photographed wildflowers, boats and birds. He searched for subjects to keep practicing photography during his off-water months.

One day about three years ago, Michael accompanied me on a late fall Sunday to Albany muni to walk with friends and their dogs.

Michael found his winter photography subjects and so began his fascination with and appreciation of the dogs at the golf course.

At first, he photographed his friends' dogs — their interactions with each other, their playful running and jostling. He captured their expressions, their personalities, their bodies, fur and coloring.

He looked around and began photographing strangers' dogs — 664 in all, so far.

Most dog walkers are pleased that someone is admiring and photographing their beloved pets. Many dogs bound up to Michael to pose and preen. He asks the dog's breed and name and explains that he will post the photos on his website and the owners may copy the photos for their own use.

Michael snaps up to 1,000 photos per outing and chooses the best to post on albanydogs.net. Owners use the pictures as screen savers, print and frame them and make them into calendars. One dog walker used the photos as jigsaw puzzles on the Jigidi website.

It made sense at first to categorize the dogs by breed. But many were mixed breeds so Michael listed them as whatever the owner said, drawing the line at two breeds. When he took subsequent photos of the same dog, some owners described their

Photos courtesy of Michael Kalin

Dr. Pepper, from the Labrador retriever page on AlbanyDogs.net

Here are some statistics from AlbanyDogs.net*:

■ **Number of dogs:** 664
■ **Number of photos:** 1,826
■ **Most popular names:** Bella and Tucker
■ **Most popular breed:** Labrador

As of April 2015

pet's heritage in a different order or combination of breeds. For ease of reference, the dogs also are indexed by names.

My original dog-walking friends and I would like to collect some of the photos in book format. The problem has been choosing which photos — and this problem has only grown as the number has multiplied.

▶ *Contributor Julie Elson lives in Albany.*

Bella kept loneliness at bay

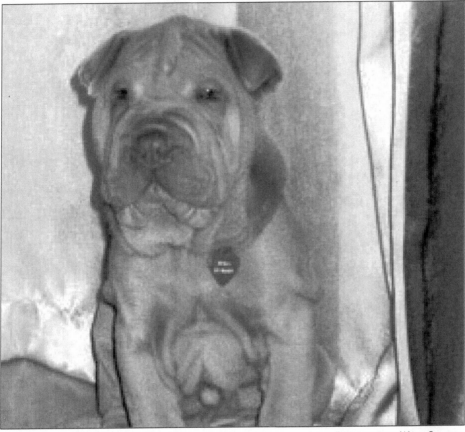

Photo courtesy of Karen Gregware

Bella, a Shar-Pei, as a puppy.

By Karen Gregware

My 9-year-old shar-pei Bella is truly a best friend and protector to me. We brought Bella home at 5 weeks old and she was the most adorable puppy, with all those wrinkles.

My husband served two tours in Afghanistan and that left me to live alone all the way across country from my family and friends. Every night, when I came home from work, she was there to show me love, listen to how my day was and protect me.

Shar-Peis are guard dogs and to this day she does just that. Without her during those 15 months, I would have been extremely lonely.

▶ *Contributor Karen Gregware lives in Green Island.*

DNA test offered clues to ZZ's mystery mix

Times Union archive

ZZ Zlotsky, who has basenji, Shetland sheepdog, American Eskimo dog and Cairn terrier genes.

By Michael Janairo

ZZ was a mystery dog. When he was adopted in 1990 from the Blackhawk Humane Society in Waterloo, Iowa, ZZ — a nickname for Zeke Zlotsky — was 6 months old and housebroken. But his lineage, his early upbringing and why he was given up were unknown.

In her first few months with him, Deborah Zlotsky, ZZ's "mom," said he often chewed up the trash and gnawed on furniture, but he was also affectionate, play-

ful and trusting with her. He weighed only about 10 pounds, so with people (but not dogs) he could be suspicious and reticent.

I first met ZZ when he was about 9 years old, and I was suspicious and reticent. I had never been a pet owner and have allergies. Dogs usually growl or bark at me, or try to jump on me and lick me, failing to respect my personal space.

All ZZ did was sniff my pant cuffs and hand. He let me pet him, and then he walked away, got a drink of water and curled up on his

bed. I liked him.

I learned that when he snorted, he was saying, "Look at me." When he stomped his front paws, he was saying, "I need to go out." And when he barked, not a yap but full-bodied and resonant like a much bigger dog's, he was telling squirrels to watch it.

On walks, ZZ introduced me to the strange secret society of dog owners who know each other by their dogs' names (Sally's mom, Bailey's dad). When people checked out ZZ's markings — black fur over his body and face, and white fur on his neck, legs, belly and a blaze on his fore-head — they asked, "What breed is he?"

"He's a mix," I said, but Deborah, now my wife (making me ZZ's stepdad), sometimes said, "He's part fox, part cat and part skunk."

The next question, "A mix of what?" had no definitive answer.

When ZZ was 18, a sample of his DNA was sent to Wisdom Panel Mx. According to Mars Veterinary, the company that developed it, the test compares a mixed-breed dog's DNA from a blood sample with a genetic database of from more than 130 breeds.

The most common guess, from a veterinary staff and Times Union readers, was that ZZ was a basenji. According to the results, ZZ's ancestry did include "a significant amount" of basenji with some Shetland sheepdog and distant traces of American Eskimo dog and cairn terrier.

Basenjis date back to Egypt in the time of the pharaohs. They are small, intelligent companions who don't bark but can howl, whine and whimper.

Deborah said ZZ's lineage links him to three continents — Africa for basenji; Europe for Shetland sheepdog and cairn terrier; and North America for the American Eskimo dog. "It makes him even more exotic than I already thought."

"He is a remarkable and

ZZ'S ANCESTRY contains a significant amount of basenji with some Shetland sheepdog and distant traces of American Eskimo dog and cairn terrier. Here is a look at the different breeds:

BASENJI: a significant amount
■ **Traits:** Athletic, intelligent, playful; aloof around strangers; chases wildlife; quick learner; doesn't bark; weighs 20-26 pounds

SHETLAND SHEEPDOG: some trace
■ **Traits:** Intelligent; alert; active; aloof with strangers; enjoys sports; may herd children; weighs 19-20 pounds

AMERICAN ESKIMO DOG: distant traces
■ **Traits:** Alert; intelligent; eager to learn; wary of strangers; weighs 6 to 40 pounds

CAIRN TERRIER: distant traces
■ **Traits:** Active; alert; can be difficult to disengage from an activity; strong-willed; may scratch at ground or dig, or chase wildlife; weighs 13-16 pounds

ZZ
■ **Traits:** Active; athletic; alert; aloof; likes to run and play; chases wildlife; doesn't bark; weighs about 10 pounds

beloved dog," ZZ's mom said, "whether I know his lineage or not."

──────────────────

▶ *Michael Janairo is a former* *Times Union arts editor. This feature is compiled from two stories that first appeared in the Times Union in March and June 2008.*

Labrador? Yes. Retriever? No.

By Jennifer Rodger

Photo courtesy of Jennifer Rodger

Ceridwyn (Cara), a black Labrador retriever.

Ceridwyn (Cara) was a gorgeous black female Labrador retriever, AKC registered and all.

Glossy black double coat, dense "otter" tail, webbed feet, she looked every part the regal gun dog. Somewhere in her genetic coding, a few twists of DNA went awry.

Theoretically a water dog, she eschewed water as if it were radioactive waste. On walks, she would tiptoe around puddles to keep those webbed toes dry. In her puppyhood, I was known to stand out in the rain, holding an umbrella over her (while I got drenched), so that she would go out and do her business. Ostensibly a gun dog, she was so terrified of loud noises that she had her own prescription of Xanax for thunderstorms, Fourth of July, and the first day of hunting season.

Prior to the pharmaceutical relief she got from her meds, I spent many a stormy night with 85 pounds of quivering dog half in my lap, half buried under the couch pillows.

And then there was retrieving. I was determined to keep my Lab happy, and bought endless tennis balls, Frisbees and retrieving dummies for her to (hopefully) retrieve with joy. At the first toss, she would lope out after the object, and bring it back with a low level of enthusiasm. The second throw was followed by a longer pause before pursuit, and a decidedly resentful return trip, culminating in an unceremonious deposit of the toy at my feet. The third? Never happened. No way, no how. "Get it yourself, lady" was clearly the message, as she would go find something better to do (napping, mostly).

Being a diligent and clearly slow-learning dog mom, I kept at it. Every few weeks I'd try to pique her interest, and countless toys littered the porch and yard. There was one Frisbee in particular, a large, floppy one, that I was convinced she'd like, because she never cared for any plastic toys.

For the record, she didn't like it. Who'd have thought?

One afternoon, I stepped out on the porch to call the dog in from the yard, and as I looked down onto the grass, I saw the aforementioned Frisbee. Smack in the middle of it was a large, steaming, fresh deposit, clearly belonging to a certain large Lab. I finally got the message. The Frisbee was tossed, and I invested in more organic dog treats instead.

▶ *Contributor Jennifer Rodger lives in Hudson.*

Sailor Bob fits in wherever he goes

Photos courtesy of John Runfola

Sailor Bob, a Shetland sheepdog.

By John Runfola

Sailor Bob was a failure at four months. His breeders hoped he would develop into a winning show dog. He had it all, the chestnut coat, white beard, floppy ears and intelligence common to all Shetland sheepdogs.

But the size of his paws barred him from any chance at a future in the ring at the Westminster Dog Show. The breeders said his paws projected an adult weight and size far out of the standard set by the American Kennel Club, the governing body of what makes a breed a breed in the United States.

So the owners had the dilemma of having to sell an aging puppy with movie star looks, but what would be a huge body, in early September, far from the traditional sales seasons.

We had just lost Maxie, our beloved sheltie, after 15 years of love and caring. She had herded our two babies to keep them away from danger and had provided countless hours of watching over her "flock." The runt of the litter, Maxie was a fearless dog at 17 pounds, often running off dogs four times her weight.

The children grew up and my wife and I grew older. Now the boys were off to law school and college. The house was very quiet.

Could we survive life without a dog?

It turned out we lasted less than a month. A picnic at Saratoga Spa State Park, with its parade of happy dogs and owners, did us in.

I got the name of a reliable local breeder from a colleague. I called and was told the next litter of shelties was due around the winter holidays. I said I didn't want to train a new puppy in the cold weather, and besides, the house would be too busy with people to give our new companion enough attention.

Then the breeder said she had an older puppy being groomed as a show dog who was too big to make the cut. Would I be interested in a male dog who might weigh 45 pounds instead of the usual 25 pounds?

I made the short trip to the kennel and that is where we met.

The breeders, expert salespeople, put the dog in an open crate. I was encouraged to pet him. He licked my hand. That was it. Love at first lick.

I had a new friend for life. I hoped my wife would approve.

Shelties are somewhat of a mixed breed, originating with farm dogs called "toonies" in the Shetland Islands. The dogs were small and had rough coats to survive the freezing weather. Their devotion was given to their flock of sheep and their masters.

Of course, the dogs ended up going on trips with the fishermen who harvested whatever they could get from the unforgiving ocean.

"Sailor Bob" was a legendary seagoing toonie who shared the dangers of each voyage with his master. As legend goes, Sailor Bob did his part to increase the population of dogs on the island. But that is another story.

Our Sailor Bob just wanted to fit in from the first time I brought him home. My wife,

Sailor Bob watching TV.

who was recovering from a serious ankle injury, had some doubts about caring for him while I was at work each evening.

That never was a problem. He has been a great friend and companion to my wife, and his protectiveness helps ease my guilt about leaving her alone so many nights. He quietly sleeps at her feet as the day nears its end.

Sailor Bob knows the way when we make our morning round of the neighborhood.

Our hourlong treks are often interrupted because many people want to stop to chat about a dog they usually call "Lassie" after the dog in the famous TV show and movies. It is also not unusual that drivers stop their cars to chat about the dog. The ham

that he is, Sailor Bob laps up the attention.

We also laugh at him during his time as an "inside dog." He loves to watch television, and of course, "Lassie Come Home" is his favorite film. He barks and jumps at the screen whenever Lassie appears. No dog or bark of a dog off-camera escapes his notice. He barks right back. He also loves "Gunga Din" with its on-the-loose elephant, and any show involving horses. He followed the chariot races in "Ben-Hur" with great interest.

Sailor Bob loves to chase what we call "Tinkerbell," when light flashes from a reflection of glass on the inside walls of our home.

He is at his best during family gatherings, when his "children" come home for a precious few days with us. He dances and barks greetings, then happily waits to see what comes next. Like all dogs, it hopefully involves food.

In many ways I think I should live my life more like Sailor Bob. He is forgiving, lives in the moment and always is up for the next adventure. He never complains and just wants to be included in whatever is going on. It has been a fast six years with Sailor Bob in our lives, and I am looking for many more good times and laughs to come.

► *Contributor John Runfola lives in Schenectady and works at the Times Union.*

The beautiful bull terrier

By Mark Schaming

There has always been a bull terrier in the house. One doesn't exactly own a bull terrier. They are delightfully unpredictable dogs who live with you, very much on their own terms.

Sylvia is as clownish, athletic and idiosyncratic as any I've known. She demands love and affection, and is baffled by a guest who doesn't share her immediate expectation of recognition and touch. She will not tolerate being ignored.

Our daughters grew up walking these magnificent animals along the sidewalks of Albany, mistaking laughter and rude pointing from strangers as enthusiastic compliments. As far as they were concerned, this was the ultimate dog by acceptable beauty standards. They'd smile proudly when a passerby would declare "pig on a leash!" or, "Is that a dog?"

To them, as with me, these lovely dogs defy the accepted standard of what is beautiful. To us, any dog with a pronounced "stop" in front of the eyes where the muzzle meets the skull is unusual. There is nothing like the expressive eyes, filled head and sure gait of a bull terrier.

Sylvia, like many bull terriers, is lovable and conflicted.

While she can decide to play beyond normal bounds, Sylvia can suddenly become bored. She craves the couch, and regularly performs a "Bully-Run" indoors, a sort of jubilant victory lap showing its human

Photo courtesy of Mark Schaming

Sylvia, the bull terrier.

family the extent of her glee. The girls knew early on to pick up their feet as she tore past, as lamps fell, tables tilted and rugs upended. This is a very present and innovative dog.

Sylvia came home with us as a promising 6-month-old show dog with a fancy registered name that we never called her. The plan was that a handler would tour her around the United States and she'd become a champion and then retire to our family full time. The ribbons came and she was pronounced a champion.

Very quickly after her show career ended, she became dedicated to digging deep holes in the yard, followed by long naps in the sun with her white face blackened.

Sylvia was never trained to sit on command. She walks triumphantly, loves the leash, stands like a chiseled figure and allows just about anyone to pet her, but will not sit or lie on command, as if it's beneath her. Say "down!" and she looks at you like you're a sucker.

Bull terriers have the reputation of being dumb but I think that is a misconception. Perhaps to some, a confident animal with tiny eyes and an egg-shaped head suggests low intelligence, but not to us. She exudes an independent demeanor, is a powerfully loving dog lost in thought with great determination.

▶ *Contributor Mark Schaming lives in Delmar.*

Zoey Peepers is a greyhound ambassador

By Laurie Wheelock

My husband, Jim, and I adopted Peepers, now named Zoey Peepers, from a greyhound racetrack in Connecticut in spring 2010.

Peepers was her race name and while the shelter joked that she was probably one of the slowest greyhounds ever to race, we could tell by looking into her big brown eyes that she was up for adventure, but maybe just not sprinting.

A sweet-natured, goofy girl, Zoey only raced actively for two weeks before she was put up for adoption. She apparently would get so distracted by all the spectators that she would walk over to the stands to get pets rather than run around the track chasing an electronic rabbit.

We scooped her up immediately and she became our four-legged best friend and adventuring partner.

It was the year I finished graduate school in Vermont. For Jim and me, that summer felt like the beginning of a whole new chapter in our lives and Zoey was ready to lead the way.

Shortly after adopting Zoey, we moved from beautiful Vermont to bustling Brooklyn. We were nervous about how Zoey would take the move but quickly saw how much she loved the big city. On our first walk through McGolrick Park in Brooklyn, four children ran

Photo courtesy of Laurie Wheelock

Zoey Peepers, a rescued greyhound.

over to meet her. She was calm and very interested in all of the attention she received. After that experience, we were surprised how many people in the big city would take time to stop and talk to us about Zoey.

She became a daily greyhound rescue dog ambassador. People were constantly approaching us and asking questions about her. How fast can she run? Is she a tiger? — she has brindle-colored fur. Is she supposed to be that skinny and muscular at the same time? Why does she

have tattoos in her ears?

We always answered people's questions and Zoey would often answer them in her own way (a roo, a lick).

Following the arrival of our son Riley, who is Zoey's biggest fan, and a job promotion, we are now living in Albany where Zoey continues to be a greyhound rescue ambassador. She is enjoying exploring her new city and meeting new people she can roo to.

▶ *Contributor Laurie Wheelock lives in Albany.*

Just Dawg never wants to be left behind

By Anne Bartol

My father loved dogs. We always had one in the house, and every time we lost one, my mother would say, "No more dogs!" Somehow, another dog always managed to appear.

My husband and I followed the same pattern — always a dog around, sometimes two. Over more than 40 years, we loved Spoochie, Eysenck, Tepla, Tasha, Tika, Zippy, Pico, Casey, and Moka — five German shepherds, one Samoyed, three lovable mutts. Now we have J.D.: part Vizsla, mostly lovable mutt.

Depending on whom you ask, J.D. stands for juvenile delinquent, Jack Daniels, juris doctor, jelly doughnut or just dawg. J.D. is my husband's boy. Curt worries about him on our overnight trips and getaway vacations. His first words as we get into the car on our way home? "We're coming, J.D."

After all, J.D. has "abandonment issues," Curt says, even after being with us for eight years. That's why he is forgiven for greeting us too wildly when we return home, whether we've been gone 15 minutes or three hours. He mopes at the sight of luggage and sighs when he senses an imminent shopping trip or evening out. Once, when we dropped him off at a kennel before leaving for a week, he jumped into the trunk of the car as I was removing his dog bed.

Photo courtesy of Anne Bartol

J.D., the lovable mutt.

And he finds ways to punish us for leaving, even for a short time. If I forget to put the right obstacles on the leather couch, there will be paw prints and dog hair on our return.

J.D. was found wandering beside a country road. He was at one shelter for eight months, and he was scheduled for the death penalty when another shelter rescued him. Curt immediately fell for this tawny, scrawny dog. The shelter manager tried to persuade us to adopt a retriever, a pit bull mix, or a beagle. "You don't want that one, he might run away." When we didn't budge, she said, "Well, at least he never barks."

J.D. barks. He barks at Mr. Brown's UPS truck. He barks when we drive into the driveway. He barks when anyone appears at the door. He barks in the background when I'm on the phone.

J.D. is a bright, sweet, com-passionate, moral dog. He's patient with kids and cats, and he tolerates that yappy little papillon our daughter adores. Curt insists he knows at least 182 words (list available on request), and he's certain J.D. would save us or any of our grandchildren in a crisis. He'd rush into a burning building, he'd charge a home invader, he'd jump into the pond (even though he hates to be immersed in water), and he'd share the last meatball. I'm skeptical, but surely he would be more helpful than the cat.

When we lose J.D., in the event we outlive him, I know I'll be tempted to say "no more dogs" as my mother did.

Let me not give in to temptation, though. We have time for at least one more dog, don't we? Besides, you meet the nicest people in the vet's office.

▶ *Contributor Anne Bartol lives in Glenville.*

A vacation flirtation becomes a commitment

By Willard Bridgham

Rodrigo in the garden at the Quinta Loreto.

During a recent visit with family in San Miguel de Allende, Mexico, we stayed at the Quinta Loreto hotel, where we met a dog we have since named Rodrigo after another new friend.

We first saw him dancing nimbly to avoid stones thrown by the protective owner of a female dog in heat. Rodrigo's cheerful attitude amused us. He glanced back at the object of his affection with undaunted optimism and trotted proudly away.

When I first petted him, I was shocked: He was so emaciated that every vertebra stood out on his back. He was friendly and polite and I was missing my own dog so we played and rested for a while in the garden.

I thought that some food would be a help to him and I went to the butcher to get some *carne* and *huesos*. His energy level improved a lot after he had eaten, as did our esteem for each other. My whole family liked him, as does everyone who meets him; he is a charming dog.

I was told that the dog officer was coming to get Rodrigo and he would be taken away and euthanized soon. I was concerned about his future. He met us at the gate the morning we left, as cheerful as ever.

Another guest at the Quinta offered to feed him and contact an organization she knew of that might send Rodrigo to us in Albany.

I clung to this hope and, when we returned to New York, I had a phone message from Irene Diamant of SPA, which rescues dogs and cats in San Miguel de Allende, and we arranged to have Rodrigo sent here. Kelly Karger of Save A Mexican Mutt and Irene made vet and boarding arrangements and Kelly transported Rodrigo to Texas to board an airplane and fly to New York.

I went to LaGuardia airport to pick up Rodrigo 1½ hours early, like an expectant father, and cooled my heels 'til he came. I feared that Rodrigo would be frightened and fearful from the airplane trip or have difficulty with a car.

Rodrigo arrived in a doggy box his usual cheerful self and greeted me pleasantly. He jumped into the car and chewed some *huesos* I brought with me and then fell asleep for the long drive home.

I worried about how Rodrigo would get along with our 6-year-old dog, Booker T.

Booker is usually good with other dogs and Rodrigo loved him at first sight. After a good romp in the backyard, they both fell asleep at the foot of my bed, nose-to-nose.

Rodrigo has integrated with our family very well and is much healthier.

My family and I are grateful to the people who helped Rodrigo and me.

▶ *Contributor Willard Bridgham lives in Albany.*

Precious lived up to her name

By Ed DerGurahian

Precious. Just the name alone tells you what we thought of her. Admittedly, I only knew Precious for a brief amount of time, as I met my wife in 2007 and we had to put Precious down in 2013. But in those six short years, she showed me unconditional love.

Let me take you back to the first time my wife met Precious. Her father had come home and announced, "I bought a dog." No one believed him until they saw a 4-month-old ball of fur that was very depressed. Precious spent her first months of life in a pet store and was nearly put down until my wife helped her through her shyness and sadness into a vibrant, healthy cocker spaniel.

When I first met Precious, it was my first weekend overnight at my now in-laws. Precious didn't take well to the fact that I was invading her territory and taking her "mommy" away. To show her gratitude, she followed me up to the room where I would be sleeping and promptly peed in the carpet. We couldn't yell at her, as we all thought that this was hilarious, so we had to show the dog that her "mommy" wasn't going anywhere — just someone else in both her and Precious' life.

Precious tolerated me for a while, but she didn't love me until I gave her food. In Precious' case, it was carrots. One year, for Christmas, I bought

Photo courtesy of Ed DerGurahian

Precious, a cocker spaniel.

her a big bag of Dole baby carrots, and they were gone in three days.

On July 4, 2010, not only was it Independence Day, but it was also the day that my wife and I were married. It was a gorgeous, hot, sun-soaked day in Glens Falls. The guys went to a golf course. The women in the bridal party arrived to get ready. There were five women in the wedding party, but of course, there were really six. Although Precious couldn't wear a dress that day, she did have a giant bow on her head that matched perfectly with the bridesmaids' gowns. If you look through our wedding album, one of the best pictures is of the women holding Precious with the bow on her head, and Precious looking as if all she wants to do is sleep.

I know that she was very happy for us, but I think she could have dealt without the commotion at her house.

About three months before we had to put her down, Precious was still the queen of the house. When my wife and I adopted a new cat, Simba, and brought him up to my in-laws' house, he would not step foot in the same room as Precious. We knew that this made Precious happy, as she had that room all to herself. But she enjoyed having Simba around, as the newness of his arrival took the attention off of her and let her sleep. Even though she was old, she was still in charge, and let everyone know it.

▶ *Contributor Ed DerGurahian lives in Menands.*

Maisy wanted to walk, so hiking became a hobby

By Jake Dillon

Declaring that I wanted to get a dog didn't go over well. The lady of the house said no more animals.

I already picked out the name, Frank, and breed and size: male Lab, 100 pounds plus.

My easy task turned into a two-year process. Mohawk Hudson Humane Society is one of the first places I searched. They had plenty of animals but I was waiting for the right one.

One day, there was a little female, described as an Australian shepherd mix.

The next day, I got in the truck and headed down. She was a good dog, playful, happy. Yes, she's the one.

My daughters named her: One liked Daisy, the other liked Mazy. Maisy it is.

Walking around the block gets real boring really fast. We spent the first few months covering all the Pine Bush trails near my home. The first 50-degree day with no snow cover, we picked more than 50 ticks from Maisy.

There were plenty of places to go: Thacher Park, Lawson Lake, Cole, Wolf, Bennett Hill are great places. Maisy loves all; I get bored quickly.

I was complaining again at work when a coworker asked why not become a 46er. I looked into what that meant and where to do it — climb the highest peaks of the Adirondacks. Cascade Mountain is

Photo couresy of Jake Dillon

Daisy, an Australian shepherd mix.

one of the shortest trails up that way. Off we went. How hard can this be?

How many times in my life have I said, "If I knew then what I know now." Route 73 was filled with cars. I took my dog, backpack, water bottles, sandwich, dog food and change of socks in case water got through my sneakers — yes, sneakers.

The number of people was surprising. It was like walking in downtown Lake George. With so many people, I kept Maisy on the leash almost the whole way up. We stayed on top for quite a while and the crowds thinned out.

Once she was off the leash, she investigated everything. We tried a few more peaks. We hiked up to the Santanoni Peak right after Hurricane Irene. I now understand what is meant by "a little muddy."

We have hiked to the top of about 100 mountains so far, almost all of the state forests and preserves in our area, 70 or so in the Catskills.

Maisy has been leading the way up and down all of the hikes. If I want to go down a different way than we came up she will sit and wait for a few minutes as if to tell me, "Hey, jackass, over here."

The day we hiked up Rusk Mountain in the Catskills was warm with lots of brush to push out of the way. I lost my GPS. Not having any idea where I lost it, I turned around and stared down what I thought was the same path. Maisy sat and waited. Just a few feet down from her was the GPS. Good dog. Really good dog.

▶ *Contributor Jake Dillon lives in Colonie.*

Honey was saved, then she saved her owner

By Margaret Donohue

My brother Peter adopted a black Lab/hound mix named Honey in July 2008.

She came from a woman who had adopted her a few months earlier from a rescue group that got Honey in Tennessee. Honey and her puppies were being shot at and the dogs were seized.

The woman who first adopted Honey had way too many dogs to handle and she asked my brother to take Honey because her other dogs were aggressive toward her and not letting her eat.

My brother loved her so. She is the most gentle, submissive, kindest dog.

Peter died suddenly in January 2009. My immediate reaction was "I have to take her and take care of her for him. He would want that."

I lived in Albany in a small apartment that had a no-dog policy. When I called my landlord and explained the situation, he said I could keep her because he knew I was a responsible owner.

So she became my dog. I was so depressed after Peter died. I cried so many nights and Honey would come to me and place herself in front of me and I would put my face on her smooth, silky head and just cry and cry.

My immediate family was now all gone — mother, father, brother.

Photo courtesy of Margaret Donohue

Honey, a black Lab/hound mix, in formal attire.

The first time I took her to the cemetery where my brother is buried, I swear she started pawing at the grave site. Now I know it could have been that her hound nose smelled another animal that might have been there, but maybe not. Maybe she sensed Peter was there?

When you have a pet, you just can't help but crack a smile when they do something cute.

And you are never alone. You have to walk them and that gets you out and you meet other people. One time, we were in the waiting room at Parkside Veterinary Hospital. Two young women came out of a room crying. One of them stopped, kneeled down by

Honey, and just pet her and cried and spoke to her. I just let her have her moment with my dog. Clearly, she had just lost pet. She needed comfort.

I decided to move back into the house where I grew up. So here we are — Honey, my cat Victor and me in the country. And it is fine.

We drive around and Honey hangs her head out the window with her long ears flopping in the breeze. So many people smile when they see her. That brings me joy.

Honey is 10 now. I dread the day she is no longer here, but until then, I kiss and hug her as much as possible.

▶ *Contributor Margaret Donohue lives in Greenville.*

Shy Maxwell won over the family

Photo courtesy of Connie Jo Fedorwich

Maxwell, a black Lab/spaniel mix.

By Connie Jo Fedorwich

After attending numerous adoption clinics in the Albany region, my son and I went to the Mohawk Hudson Humane Society on Jan. 20, 2015, looking for a puppy.

They had a litter of four dogs that had come up from South Carolina the day before.

A 4-month-old male black Lab/spaniel mix was in a pen with his brother. The dog, who the humane society had named Jefferson, was so timid that when they brought him out into the yard, he hid under a chair and wouldn't interact with us.

The worker at Mohawk Hudson kept telling us Jefferson would come out of his shell once he was home with us.

After an hour and a half, the dog would finally take a treat from my son but not from me.

We left, deciding that we had to think about it.

We got as far as Rensselaer and my husband, who didn't really want a dog, called to see where we were. I told him that we were bringing Jefferson home. He said we were not ready to have a dog as we didn't have dishes, food, a bed, etc.

After hearing his reaction, I decided to turn the car around and adopt Jefferson, who we renamed Maxwell.

Once home, Maxwell warmed up to me, but was timid around my son and husband for about a week. He is now the best dog. He is warm, loving, playful, and loves walks, car rides and the cat. There has not been a day that we have regretted adopting him. Even my husband loves him and is glad we got Maxwell.

▶ *Contributor Connie Jo Fedorwich lives in East Greenbush.*

Happy never left her foster home

By Stacy Horwitz

Happy was a rat terrier mixed puppy born in Florida.

Originally, she was adopted by a college student who sometimes kept her in a crate or in diapers to handle the normal business that puppies and dogs need to do on a daily basis.

Three years later, when he was about to graduate, the student didn't want Happy any longer and agreed to send her north to be fostered, retrained and eventually adopted by a loving, responsible family.

After finally being spayed and vetted with all her necessary shots, Happy arrived as a foster dog at my home in Saratoga County in 2005. Happy was just 3 years old and her name was appropriate, since her little tail never stopped wagging. She loved being held, sitting on your lap while watching TV, rewarding everyone with kisses, snuggling in your arms in bed and falling to sleep with little grunts of contentment.

Her picture with a description was posted at various veterinary hospitals, shelters and other rescue groups, but when someone finally decided to adopt her, she had already slipped into our hearts and was so loved by us that it became impossible to let her go.

Sometimes being a foster for unwanted animals is a

Happy, the rat terrier mix.

Photo courtesy of Stacy Horwitz

hard task — whether to adopt them to a good home or to keep one of them ourselves, continuing to gain hundreds of hours of unconditional love and devotion that such a sweet little dog can give. After much soul-searching, we decided not to let her go.

Happy was my beloved friend for almost 11 years before she started having medical problems. Even though she was stoic and in pain, her tail never stopped wagging. Our veterinarians and their tech staff couldn't believe how she continued to kiss everyone and still be her Happy little self, even though she was extremely ill.

Happy died during an operation to remove what turned out to be cancerous growths. She was a trouper to the very end, giving kisses and wagging her little tail for everyone who was trying to help her.

There isn't a day that goes by since her death Oct. 7, 2014, that I don't cry and miss her.

I am happy that she is no longer in pain, and know that while she was with us she had years of loving care and my unconditional love and devotion. I am so glad I had almost 11 years with my little angel dog named Happy.

▶ *Contributor Stacy Horwitz lives in Charlton.*

The new puppy needed a name that suited her

By Holly McKenna

Our third dog is our first puppy. She didn't have a name for a few days after we adopted her from the Mohawk Hudson Humane Society.

We like to pick names based on famous people and we couldn't think of a good one for our shiny, jet-black Lab mix. She has a little white on her paws and chin and a white diamond on her chest. Her soft brown eyes love to look into your eyes with complete trust and adoration.

She came to us a month after we lost our beagle Chester Arthur, named for the 21st president, who is buried in Albany Rural Cemetery. That dog was a rescue, so we didn't know his birth date. We gave our dog the same birthday as a the president and my oldest son, Oct. 5. We had Chester for 13 years.

Chester replaced our first dog Rupert Murdoch, jokingly named for the owner of the New York Post, where my husband and I worked as reporters. Rupert was a collie and German shepherd mix who lived with us for 15 years.

Our new puppy is full of life and extraordinarily curious about her surroundings. She sticks her nose into people's business and gets under their feet at every turn. Every time a dog barks on TV, she stares at the screen. Our other dogs never paid attention to most

Photo courtesy of Holly McKenna

Nellie Bly, a black Lab mix.

"people-focused" things. This dog connects with everyone and everything. Sometimes, her sense of curiosity can be a joy and curse.

We have to remind ourselves she is only a puppy and is highly intelligent. Her interest in everything also has to do with the fact that she is a social dog who loves to meet new people and animals.

Our puppy went a week without a name. It was a family joke that she would just be called "dog" or "puppy." Eventually, it was our puppy's curiosity that drove us to name her Nellie Bly, after the 19th-century investigative reporter of the same name.

For one story, the real Nellie Bly (the pen name of Ameri-

can journalist Elizabeth Jane Cochrane) did a 72-day trip around the world. For another, she disguised herself as a mental patient to find out about the deplorable living conditions at an insane asylum.

We also liked the name Nellie because it sounds Southern. Our dog was a rescue from a litter in North Carolina. In addition, Nell is the middle name of one of my Southern aunts, who has black Labs.

The name just fit her perfectly. Our Nellie Bly will never become a muckraker, but her curious nature will keep us on our toes and protect us from any harm.

▶ *Contributor Holly McKenna lives in Albany.*

Jenna doesn't judge, she simply loves

By Thalia Mossidus

Jenna came to my former husband and me 15 years ago after we lost our first dog to cancer in 2000.

I was not all that ready to adopt again, but he was, so he went online and found her at the Columbia Green Humane Society. Her name was Marcie, but she was no Marcie. I took one look at that face and those white-tipped paws and knew she was ours.

Jenna is a Lab mix and very good natured. What caught our eye at the shelter was that she would lie straight out, looking as if she were flying like Superman with her back legs extended. It was funny to see.

We brought her home that February 2000 when the snow was high. At 14 weeks, we could barely see her — it was a good thing she was black.

Through the years, she has been a wonderful dog. She has gone through a lot and in the first seven years of her life had four surgeries, two on her back legs due to arthritis, one on a mass in her neck, two on her tail due to a mass on her tail. A week later, she had to have her tail removed as the blood supply had died and so she has a stump for a tail.

Since then, my husband and I have parted ways. We had no children but Jenna and Dusty, our second dog, are my babies.

Photo courtesy of Thalia Mossidus

Jenna, a Lab mix, at 14 months old.

They are inseparable. If I take one to the vet and leave one behind, the other is waiting by the door when we come home.

Jenna has aged gracefully and I keep her comfortable, giving her all she needs. She is a little stiff these days and needs help sometimes getting up the stairs, but that's OK. I will be there for her like she's been there for me all these years, when things were not always so good.

I don't know what I would have done without her and I dread the day when I will have to say goodbye to my girl. There will never be another Jenna.

These animals ask very little in return for the unconditional love they give us. They don't judge us, they are always happy to see us. What they give us it priceless.

▶ *Contributor Thalia Mossidus lives in Scotia.*

Frank and Quinton had more room in their hearts

By Jessica Fisher Neidl

Photos courtesy of Jessica Fisher Neidl

Frank wears a life vest, left, and Quinton in the leaves.

When our dog Frank died, we both thought that our ability to love like that went with him.

We had told each other that we'd wait to adopt another dog — that we'd comfort ourselves by doing the things we'd thought about doing while we had him, that we'd travel, enjoy dog hair-free couches, come and go without having anyone but each other to take care of.

We planned to wait a year. We made it about six weeks.

After a few weeks of looking, we noticed a little brown dog named Quinn. He was the right age, the right size, the right amount of hound. But his description said he had to go to an all-female home because he was terrified of men, so we skipped over Quinn for a week or so. Something kept pulling us back. I sent an email to the rescue group.

Puppies don't know anything about life, but an adult rescue has seen a lot and is probably more wizened and world-weary than most people. When you adopt a rescue, especially one with a history of abuse and neglect, you make a promise that you'll spend every day he's with you making up for every painful, hungry, thirsty, sad, scary, lonely moment he endured, and that all he'll know in his life with you are love and kindness.

Based a note from our vet, Quinn's foster mom, Gayle, agreed to meet us.

When Gayle pulled up to our house, Quinn crouched nervously in a travel crate . We welcomed them inside, and Quinn explored the house. We took him for a walk in the park, just Bill and me. He was a good boy, a good little walker. I could see from the way Bill held the leash that he was happy.

"I think this is our dog, Babe," I said, about 30 yards out.

"I think so, too."

Though Quinn was still a stranger to us, we knew his name didn't fit. It was too soft, and he was sharp. Sharp edged, sharp eyed, angular, almost foxy. So we tacked on a syllable and he became Quinton, a dignified little man.

Quinton's fur wasn't pleasant to look at or touch. He cowered from petting.

Over time, his fur cleared, and the quirky Quintonian bald spots filled in.

Other parts of Quinton started to fill out with new softness. He stopped cowering, let us hold him and kiss his face. When we tell him we love him, he emits a sigh that sounds an awful lot like a contented "I'm home."

In the first few months we had Quinton, I worried that I'd never love him the way we loved Frank. I didn't want to love him deeply because I was sure it would be some sort of betrayal of the bond we had with our first, beloved boy.

But I was wrong. Somewhere along the line we fell in love with Quinton. We let ourselves do it. It was a relief, a new joy, our family.

▶ *Contributor Jessica Fisher Neidl lives in Albany.*

Homeless canines come from Russia for love

Photos by John Carl D'Annibale / Times Union

Mishka in her favorite chair at her new home in Delanson.

By Rebecca Landcastle

For most, a trip across the world means a business trip or a vacation. For a furry dog named Mishka, the journey from Sochi, Russia, to the Capital Region means a new beginning.

Mishka, a 5-month-old spaniel Lab/whippet mix formerly known as Liza, arrived March 20, 2015, in the United States. She is one of many rescued by Sochi Dogs, a nonprofit, volunteer-run organization dedicated to rescuing as many stray dogs from Sochi as their resources will allow.

As the 2014 Winter Olympics in Sochi approached, thousands of stray dogs wandered the city's streets, an issue that grew steadily over the years because residents abandoned pets without punishment and the city had no regulations for sterilization.

Ahead of the 2014 Winter Olympics, the city hired a company, Basya Services, to kill the stray dogs. The most common killing method was to shoot the dogs with poisoned darts.

People tried to protect dogs taken off the streets and dentist Vlada Provotorova built a shelter to protect the animals. A story about the rescue efforts in the Boston Globe spurred Anna Umansky of New Jersey to reach out to Provotorova. The rescue group had been using PayPal to collect money to buy supplies they needed to run their shelter. Umansky and others put together a fundraiser and Sochi Dogs was born in February 2014. Rescue efforts continued even after the Olympics ended, although many lost interest in helping once the games were over. "We're still there and the problem still exists," Umansky said.

Mishka was the first of the Sochi Dogs sent to the Capital Region. Peppertree Rescue, a nonprofit organization in Albany since 1998, places dogs in foster homes until they are adopted. The group is part of the Mayor's Alliance for NYC's Animals, a nonprofit umbrella organization for animal welfare in New York City.

When Mishka's potential adoption fell through, the alliance reached out to rescue groups for help and Peppertree answered.

The dog arrived at JFK airport and spent a few nights with Umansky in New Jersey.

"She was definitely nervous when she got here," Umansky said. "It was her first time being in a home."

Slowly, Mishka came out of her shell and discovered more about the new world around her. She learned that couches were comfortable for sitting and that if she sat on someone's lap they would pet her.

"Seeing her go through that process of discovery was really great and really rewarding," Umansky said.

Mishka was brought to Albany, where she was placed in foster care with Eden Roehr in Waterford. Although she was shy around the family and skittish around their other animals, the dog opened up and has great household manners, Roehr said.

Mishka began a two-week trial period with Bryan and Andrea Salisbury in Delanson.

Lex Murphy said Peppertree Rescue requires a

Andrea and Bryan Salisbury and their dogs Mishka, rescued from Sochi, Russia, and Reggie.

two-week trial before a family adopts a dog. The dog could be sent back sooner if it doesn't work out, or the trial period could be extended if they need more time to make a decision.

"The advantage of a trial period is it may or may not work, and we always learn something," Murphy said. "Whether it works or doesn't work, it's not a failure; it's what we can learn."

Mishka got her name when Bryan Salisbury started using the Russian name for Michael or Michela because it means "cuddly bear." The family said her ears perk up at the sound of her new name.

"She's probably used to hearing Russian," Andrea Salisbury said. "If you say 'Mishka,' she's right there."

The Salisburys said Mishka's introduction to the family couldn't have gone any

better. Perhaps most excited about her arrival was Reggie, the family's Lab/pit bull mix, which Murphy helped them adopt about five years ago when she was working with Homeward Bound Dog Rescue in Schenectady. The Salisburys call Mishka his "mail-order bride," and the two are already inseparable. Puppies aren't in the future for the furry couple, as Reggie is neutered and Mishka will be spayed when she is old enough.

The family already is in love with Mishka and said there's no trial about it — she's found her forever home — 5,319 miles away.

"We've adopted her," Andrea Salisbury said. "We don't have any intention of giving her back."

▶ *This story originally ran in the Times Union in April 2015.*

Living the life of Riley

By Dennis Yusko

Damian Strohmeyer / Animal Planet

Animal Planet's 11th annual Puppy Bowl. Below, Maddux, aka Bubba, who was rescued and starred in the Puppy Bowl.

One of the stars of the 2015 Puppy Bowl XI bounced around his adopted home in Lake George and landed in the arms of his owner, Michelle Maskaly.

Touchdown!

Life wasn't always so sweet for Maddux, a Chihuahua-rat terrier mix who lived in central Florida and was known as Bubba. His original owners abandoned him, his parents and seven siblings at a shelter when the pup was just 5 weeks old. The dogs had heartworm and faced uncertain futures.

But thanks to the kindness of strangers, Bubba was rescued, became Maddux, and went from rags to riches. In the fall of 2014, Animal Planet drafted the pup to play in its 11th Puppy Bowl. He was among 55 rescue dogs from across the nation that the cable channel cast to play.

The dog's good fortune did not end there. In October, during the taping of the two-hour competition, he met Maskaly, a dog lover from Lake George and Puppy Bowl volunteer.

She melted when she saw his big, round eyes and decided to adopt him on the spot.

"It was kind of like love at first sight," Maskaly said.

The Puppy Bowl is Animal Planet's takeoff on the Super Bowl and is aired before the big game. An extremely rough approximation of a football game, the Puppy Bowl was created to highlight dog rescue groups and the animals they save. The 2015 game pit Team Ruff against Team Fluff.

"I feel like rescue dogs get a bad rap sometimes," Maskaly said. "Animal Planet is really showing the amazing abilities these dogs have."

Maskaly, 35, works as an editorial director for a Chicago-based magazine. Her friend Laurie Johnson directs Florida Little Dog Rescue in St. Cloud, Fla., which saves neglected dogs. The group rescued Maddux and his family from a shelter. Maskaly met Bubba/Maddux while volunteering to clean up after the dogs while they were playing on the Animal Planet set.

Johnson trained Maddux at her home. His brothers, Steve and Pudge, also made the Puppy Bowl starting lineups.

Maskaly said all of the dogs that play on Puppy Bowl become TV stars, but she felt more pride in the rescues. "It's a privilege to hold the end of his leash," she said of her dog.

Maskaly renamed him after retired Atlanta Braves pitcher Greg Maddux. He gets along splendidly with her 7-year-old Chihuahua, Toby.

Lori Van Buren / Times Union

Johnson said she was pleased the dog was living the high life in the upstate resort.

"He went from living outside to a shelter to a foster home to the Puppy Bowl to a beautiful house in Lake George, going hiking and kayaking and playing in the snow," Johnson said. "It's kind of the whole Annie, Life of Riley-type story."

▶ *This story originally ran in the Times Union in January 2015.*

Zoeë taught a farm girl about animals

By Linnea Andersson-Wintle

When we brought her home, she was a small ball of brown sugar fluff — she was not a spontaneous pet store purchase, but one well-intended, however ignorant of the harsh realities of pet store purchases.

Zoeë, as she was soon named, would change our lives. We didn't know that at the time — at that special moment she was just a little dog.

Zoeë immediately needed us and we quickly fell in love with her. She was tiny and dependent and afraid to step on the grass outside, but would sit or stand on my foot when taken out to do her business.

I was raised on a farm. My parents taught me that animals were to be treated with respect and kindness, but that farm animals had jobs to do and a purpose to fulfill. Still, I mourned them when they were sold or came to their logical farm end.

Now along came this little Pomeranian puppy who taught me there was much more to an animal. She taught me that dogs have souls and hearts that break, that they forgive and most importantly, love.

Zoeë was 10 weeks old when she came to our family. She was to be the family dog, but she quickly attached to me. I could never have imagined the special bond that formed

Photo courtesy of Linnea Andersson-Wintle
Linnea Andersson-Wintle with Zoeë, the Pomeranian.

between us. She was by my side always. She followed me to the bathroom and waited patiently outside the shower or by my feet if possible. If I sat in a chair and moved, her little head was up and her beautiful black almond-shaped eyes followed me to see if I was going to get up. Her brown sugar color grew into a lovely tan and she grew into an elegant and regal girl. When I returned home from anywhere, she was right at the door to greet me as if I had been gone forever.

At times, my husband would let her wait on the lawn for me. She never moved from her spot until she heard my car and only then she got up, but didn't move until I safely motioned her into the

car and onto my lap.

She died too soon — quietly, from congestive heart failure at the age of 10. I grieved for her companionship, devotion, her sweetness and her ever presence. But she left a legacy. I learned about puppy mills and dog rescue and became a rescue transporter. My daughter became a transporter and, in turn, her mother-in-law.

To honor Zoeë's memory, I adopted a rescue Pomeranian who had roamed the streets as a stray. My heart and my life are richer and more joyful because of a little Pom named Zoeë.

▶ *Contributor Linnea Andersson-Wintle lives in Guilderland.*

Koko the chocolate Lab helps 3 generations

By Renee Bernard

My dog Koko has captured my heart and those of many people who have come in contact with her.

She is a chocolate Lab and was born July 3, 2006. My son, Nick, wanted a chocolate Lab after seeing one in a store.

My father had been diagnosed with Alzheimer's and my mother was at the late stages of cancer. Her oncologists said I should get a dog — it would be good for me as well for as my sick parents.

We went to a large farm in Endicott, Broome County, where we were greeted by a huge male dog, the father of the litter. In a large crate were four little female Labs, tuckered out from playing all day. One of them immediately came out of the crate and went to my son. You could say she picked us.

My father had been against getting a puppy but when we brought her home, she went right to him as if she knew something was wrong. He picked her up and placed her on the end table next to him and pet her. From that day forward, he pet and fed her when no one was looking.

He called her Koko-Beanie, his "little brown-eyed girl." To this day, my father knows her name but none of his children's. He is a Korean War vet and lives at the Teresian

Photo courtesy of Renee Bernard

Koko, the chocolate Lab, with Renee Bernard and her father, Richard Bernard.

House memory care floor, which allows families and the nurses to bring in their pets. That makes my father very happy.

Sometimes when I look at Koko, it's like she looks into my soul. I once told my veterinarian, Dr. Lara Patrick, that Koko means more to me than my family does and she laughed and said, what if your family heard you say that? I told her they already knew.

▶ *Contributor Renee Bernard lives in Loudonville and works at the Times Union.*

Ziggy can do math, read – Jenna is still learning

By Terry Brown

Ziggy and Jenna, 7-year-old shelties, team with me in my role as an Albany Airport Ambassador to serve passengers and staff.

Both are certified Canine Good Citizen dogs and Therapy Dog International canines. They are on the lookout for passengers in need of therapy, release from the stresses of travel and grief from the loss of a relative or a friend.

Ziggy and Jenna are two of 22 Albany International Canine Customer Service Ambassadors. Each of 18 handler-canine teams are ready to visit passengers having concerns. The team gets cleared by Transportation Security Administration officers for duty on the second floor where passengers await flights.

Ziggy and Jenna interact with more than 100 people each tour. They welcome and encourage petting.

Ziggy is a mathematician, can read 13 words and do simple tricks on command. Jenna watches and learns.

When I hold up a piece of paper that has "sit," "down" or "roll over," Ziggy follows the written command. He can count to 20, add, subtract, multiply, divide and even calculate square roots.

During a recent tour, I walked the dogs up to several children and asked, "Do you want to help Ziggy do his math homework?" "Sure,"

Paul Buckowski / Times Union

Terry Brown and his two dogs, Ziggy, left, and Jenna visit with children at Franklin D. Roosevelt Elementary School in Schenectady during an award ceremony for Brown in March.

the kids responded.

"How old are you?" I asked. The youngster responded "3."

"Ziggy, are you ready to count?" He sat down and I said, "Count to 3." Ziggy placed a paw in my hand three times. I asked the child's sister, "How old are you?" She said "4."

"Count to 4, Ziggy." He did. "Ziggy, how much is 3 and 4?" He counted to 7. He subtracted 4 from 7 and counted to 3. He answered 2 times 2 is 4. He divided 3 into 6 and answered 2.

A woman said she was sad because her 9-year-old Lab was hit by a truck and killed two days earlier. As the woman knelt to pet Ziggy, she smiled as he licked her face.

Once, we spotted a woman with tears in her eyes. She said she was sad because she missed her pet dog, in a kennel for two weeks until her return.

After Ziggy did a couple of his tricks, he left her happier.

Many passengers ask what dogs are doing in the airport. Sometimes I respond by telling them, "They're your pilots" or "They're sniffing for an extra lunch." I always warn them Jenna likes coffee.

Several parents requested Ziggy and Jenna visit with their children as a distraction to their fear of flying.

We end our shift in the Capt. John McKenna Military Courtesy Room.

Ziggy and Jenna also help a reading program at an elementary school in Schenectady and provide therapy to nursing home residents in Clifton Park.

▶ Contributor Terry Brown lives in Latham and is a regular Times Union contributor.

Robby had the right stuff after all

By Christy Ann Coppola

Robby was born at Guiding Eyes for the Blind. He was supposed to become a working service dog. However, after several critical evaluations, the team knew that Robby simply didn't have the right stuff for guide work, so he was put up for public adoption.

In fact, his entire litter, with the exception of one puppy, was released. After being on the waiting list for two years, I got the call that they had a puppy for me. I headed down to Yorktown Heights to pick up my 11-week-old bundle of yellow Labrador.

He was as quiet as a church mouse, and, even during the three-hour ride back to Clifton Park, he didn't make a peep. He was curled up in his crate in the back of my SUV and as I glanced back at him, I knew that I had a special little pup on my hands.

As a dog trainer myself and a past puppy raiser for GEB, I raised Robby as if he were going to be a guide. I gave him plenty of socialization, exposure training, obedience and life skills.

When Robby became a young adult he passed his Canine Good Citizen test and shortly thereafter became a registered therapy dog.

Since then, we have become a very active visiting team. We regularly participate in the reading program

Photo courtesy of Christy Ann Coppola

Robby visiting with his friend Alex.

at the Clifton Park Library, visit nursing homes and hospitals, and college students during finals week. But the biggest impact Robby has made is visiting with special needs children.

For the past three years we have worked closely with the staff at Okte Elementary School. Robby visits with children with autism, some on the far end of the spectrum. The change in these children is remarkable. Some who were noncommunicative are now speaking, saying Robby's name, pointing to pictures, and even carrying themselves differently. One boy we met was petrified of dogs, but sitting quietly with Robby in the room has not only built this child's confidence, but has allowed him to get over his fear of dogs. By the second week he had whispered "I love you"

in Robby's ear.

The feedback from parents is truly touching and makes me realize that although Robby didn't fulfill his goal of becoming a guide dog, he is making a huge impact in the lives of many, right here in the Capital Region, and that makes me extremely proud.

Working with Robby has allowed me to meet people I normally wouldn't have the opportunity to meet, and as a transplant from NYC, it has helped me feel like I'm part of the community. I'm thrilled that Robby is able to join me in giving back.

When we aren't working, Robby's favorite activities include playing fetch, swimming and hiking at Kinns Road Park in Clifton Park.

▶ *Contributor Christy Ann Coppola lives in Clifton Park.*

Brandi knew how to work the crowd

By Linda DeLong

Brandi stole our heart the minute we looked into those puppy blue eyes.

As many times as we were warned about chocolate Labs and their mood swings, we couldn't resist those eyes that said, "Take me home."

Although at times I wished I had listened, she was the best in spite of her loose screw, as I called it.

One day, when Brandi was about 6 months old, she went from resting quietly on the floor as my friend and I watched television to jumping up, running around in circles and going airborne onto our laps. She knocked off my friend's glasses, then jumped back down to the floor for a couple more spins before she plopped down and went back to sleep. These episodes became the norm.

In spite of that loose screw, Brandi went on to become a therapy dog like none other. The more places we took her, the more calls we would get for requests for her to visit. She would walk into a facility and immediately take over. An award from the state Senate recognized Brandi along with police dogs for community service.

Since breaking her from jumping was an impossible task, we put a command to it that pleased the people we were visiting and satisfied her need to jump. I would say, "Brandi, do you want to

Photo courtesy of Linda DeLong

Brandi, the chocolate Lab, as a puppy.

dance?" and immediately both paws landed on my shoulders with a look that said, "Thanks, Mom, I needed that."

With that out of her system, she went about her business — working the crowd and making people think she loved them best. She went to hospitals, nursing homes, schools, private homes and birthday parties and loved every minute of it.

At the age of 7, Brandi was diagnosed with a very aggressive cancer and in less than a week we were faced with what every loving dog owner dreads — putting her to sleep.

At the vet's office, they brought her into a makeshift living room, her head hung down and she was having trouble breathing from the growth pressing on her windpipe, but she never missed a beat.

She greeted the doctor, vet tech and family members one by one with her whole body wagging, doing what Brandi always did best — working the crowd.

Had I known that day I looked into those puppy blue eyes that her life was going to be cut short and I would have to say good-bye so quickly, I still wouldn't have changed a thing.

We learned so much from her and she left us with so many beautiful memories. Our beautiful, arrogant, independent and fun-loving chocolate Lab with a loose screw.

Her job was done.

▶ *Contributor Linda DeLong lives in Valatie.*

Daisy taught owner how to move on after breakup

By Maria Geizer

"**A**t some point, a dog just starts to do what she is supposed to do." Someone once told me this, in the midst of the rigors of puppyhood, for which I was a novice and wholly unqualified. My source of stress was a tiny ball of black fluff and gumption, a mix of shepherd, beagle and border collie who I named Daisy before we even decided to bring her home.

I got Daisy when she was weeks old, weighing in at about a pound, if that. How this tiny being who needed no clothes, formula or college fund could wreak so much havoc in one household still mystifies me, but wreak havoc she did, in the mangled, chewed forms of shoes, sweaters, two pairs of prescription glasses, the carpet of an entire stair, vertical blinds, a tube of sunscreen and one family Christmas photo.

I'd gladly live through all of this again, knowing now what the end result would be.

I'm proud to report that, in fact, she did become a terrific dog, thanks to the efforts of both myself and my former husband.

We had no children together, and focused our love and attention on her.

She was both sweet and stubborn (the shepherd and beagle) and ruled the roost (the border collie). She was incredibly vocal; nothing made me happier than hearing

Photo courtesy of Maria Geizer

Daisy, a mix of shepherd, beagle and border collie.

her howl along with passing sirens.

And she was always portly, regardless of her diet, which was admittedly not great — she was strongly against health food of any sort.

"She's a barrel," a friend commented.

"She's thick," said another.

Daisy was perfect and soft and cuddly. Life was blissful, easy for a time, though that didn't last for me, and my marriage and life as I knew it ended sadly.

I was the lucky one who kept Daisy with me and I know now how this saved me.

I still remember the first time we walked past my former home. Daisy, trotting happily along, walked right

past without ever looking back, and continued on until we got to the door of our new, temporary place.

With my heart in my throat, I walked her in, went up to my room, and burst into tears. I was both relieved and sad, and I knew that she had just taught me what it was to move on. I was not ready, but Daisy was, and she would continue to guide me through new situations, always showing me what really matters in life: a warm bed, a belly rub and some really good snacks. And love. Lots of it. Love freely, openly and without expectation. You will be rewarded.

▶ *Contributor Maria Geizer lives in Saratoga Springs.*

Volunteers turn puppies into guide dogs

By Paul Grondahl

When Sheri Cross walks Baxter, a 14-month-old yellow Labrador retriever, through The Crossings of Colonie, the dog elicits smiles from walkers, bikers and joggers.

But when Baxter tries to jump up to greet a stranger or scooches exuberantly in a circle, Cross voices a heel command. She reminds well-meaning passersby that the adolescent canine is in training to become a working service dog who will assist a visually impaired or blind person.

"He's doing very well with his training and knows 18 commands, but I always have to be alert and anticipate what will become distractions for him," said Cross, a volunteer with the Guiding Eyes for the Blind's puppy-raising program.

The Keller family of Guilderland is raising their second puppy, Michael, a 9-month-old black Lab, who already weighs 75 pounds. Their previous dog was paired with a blind man.

"That little twinge in our hearts went away when we closed the circle and saw how we had helped a blind person gain independence," said Teresa Keller, a teacher at Lynwood Elementary School who brings the puppies to school.

Keller's 16-year-old daughter, Stephanie, a junior at Guilderland High School, is taking primary responsibility for the dog as community service.

Photo courtesy of Guiding Eyes for the Blind
Volunteer puppy raiser Sheri Cross gives a command to Baxter, a Labrador retriever, she is training for Guiding Eyes for the Blind.

"The work our volunteer puppy raisers do is simply priceless," said Michelle Brier, marketing manager for the Guiding Eyes for the Blind. The $45,000 cost of breeding, raising, preparing, training and supporting a Guiding Eyes team would be considerably higher without the unpaid puppy raisers. They receive training, and the dogs' veterinary bills are covered, but volunteers pay for dog food. They also make a 16-month commitment of time to walk, train and socialize the puppy.

For the Crosses, the hardest part will come when they turn over Baxter. "When we went into it, we realized we were raising a dog for someone else and we've always had that mindset," Cross said.

Learn more about Guiding Eyes for the Blind at https://www.guidingeyes.org or call 800-942-0149.

▶ *This story originally ran in the Times Union in March 2011.*

Ripley's will to live gave her extra years

By Jeanne Haug

Our beautiful puppy Ripley came to live with us on May 7, 1998. She was our daughter and we took her everywhere.

She walked the neighborhood with us, stopping to meet someone and get petted. She went to parks, hiked, swam, camped and even shopped.

We took the 120-pound, furry black Newfoundland to obedience school for seven years, earning her Canine Good Citizen, Companion Dog and Rally titles, but mostly to visit all the other dog owners. As a therapy dog, she visited the local nursing home more than 150 times.

From the beginning, we fell in love. I would look into her deep brown eyes, rub noses with her, and tell her how much I loved her. I would wrap my arms around her and hug her. I would gently blow on her nose and she'd give me a warm slobbery kiss that filled me with all of her love. No dog owner could feel more love from their dog than I did from Ripley.

As I walked in the room, she'd smile her big goofy grin at me, wag her tail, and woof for me to pet her. And I always made time to pat her on the head and give her a kiss.

At age 1½, when she began to limp, we discovered she had Lyme disease, a torn ACL and hip dysplasia. I was sick with fear that we'd be told to put her down. Each time she

Photo courtesy of Jeanne Haug

Ripley, a Newfoundland, with Ryan Haug.

survived, we were thrilled.

One day, she hit her back on the doggy door and wouldn't get up for a whole day. We worried, but yet again she came back. Even at age 12, she was exhausted from a long car ride and could barely walk. I thought she was done walking, but two days of rest, and she was back on her feet. Her will to live always brought her back.

I truly believe that she loved us as much as we loved her, that she wanted to be with us, and that she completed our lives. She showed us all how to love, how to give to her, because of what she gave to us. She'd bark, and we'd take the time to include her.

I believe her purpose in life was to bring a smile to my face, and to everyone she met. I always knew that one day she'd be gone, but I never imagined how empty I would feel. I never imagined how empty our home would feel.

At night, I'd give her a hug and a kiss and say good night. The hardest one was the final kiss goodbye as she closed her eyes for the last time. She didn't say goodbye, just drifted off to sleep. My heart broke into a million little pieces.

I am so grateful that I shared 13 years with Ripley.

▶ *Contributor Jeanne Haug lives in Clifton Park.*

Jasper gave freedom to boy and his parents

By Heather Kennison

Jasper was a black Labrador retriever. He was born, bred, raised and trained by Guiding Eyes for the Blind. He graduated from the Heeling Autism program in 2010 and was placed with our family as our son's service dog.

Jasper became the greatest gift we ever received. He saved our family.

Our son has autism and bolts away. Jasper kept our son safe in ways we could only dream of. They would be tethered to each other and any time our son would try to bolt, Jasper would lock up and pull in the opposite direction in order to keep our son from running off. Jasper alleviated a lot of stress we had to endure any time we went out. He gave us our freedom back. He also proved to be a true friend to our son — keeping secrets safe and providing many laughs with his amazing personality and animated eyebrows. He taught my son that not everyone will judge you and that you can find the best of friends in the most unexpected places. He was truly man's best friend.

We received devastating news in 2014. Jasper had lymphoma. He had only a few short months left. To have him in our lives was a blessing; the thought of him being gone so suddenly was too painful to bear. We had to make sure the time he had left with us was full of great memories.

Photo courtesy of Heather Kennison
Jasper, the black Lab, with Heather Kennison's son Tony.

We made lots of visits to parks and friends' houses. We started feeding him home-cooked meat that we mixed with food donated from Honest Kitchen. He started his medical treatments and appeared to be doing OK.

Heeling Autism let us know we would be able to receive a successor. We immediately said yes. There would be an overlap time where we would have both dogs with us. We felt it would be good, both for our son and for Jasper, to have a playmate during this difficult time.

We introduced Kodiak to our family and it couldn't have been a better match. Kodiak became our son's service dog, Jasper was retired from being a working dog and became our family dog. We had them both for six short days. We had no idea that Jasper was hanging on and waiting to know that our son would be taken care of and that he had completed his job. Even during his most severe trial, his first concern was always our son.

Jasper was a great dog, a true friend and our hero. He is greatly missed.

▶ *Contributor Heather Kennison lives in Watervliet.*

Abby helped heal the wounds of 9/11

By Chelsea Lattanzio

Most people remember their first dog, and mine is no exception. Abby was actually my mom's dog and she had a purpose.

My mother happened to be stuck in the tragic events of Sept. 11, 2001. She was across the street from the World Trade Center when the first plane hit and witnessed a lot of terrifying sights. For years after she battled with post-traumatic stress disorder. Just the sound of a fighter jet flying overhead would bring her to tears. And then one day she brought home Abby.

Abby was a Yorkshire terrier, small and full of love. Every time you walked through the front door, she would smile at you and wag her tail so hard you would think her butt would lift off the ground.

She would lie with you when you were sad, dance with you when you were feeling silly, and give you a kiss when you needed one most.

She guarded my mother and my daughter like she was the Secret Service. Above all, she always made everyone laugh.

She was needed to fix the pieces, and she did a better job at that than anyone ever could. She recently passed away, and there is not a day that goes by that we don't think about her and miss her. World's best dog.

▶ *Contributor Chelsea Lattanzio lives in Colonie.*

Photo courtesy of Chelsea Lattanzio

Abby, the Yorkshire terrier.

Dogs, like their owners, are creatures of habit

By Maryanne Malecki

I am a creature of habit. Certain routines border on ritual: the preparation of morning coffee the night before, the route to work, the household puttering and cooking reserved for Sundays.

Rhythm and structure dispense an illusory quality of order, even calm, to an increasingly disrupted life.

While some of my habits are long-standing, the structure they provide has become more obviously necessary to me as I cope with life's curveballs.

I acquired a canine roommate a bit more than 20 years ago. Tess, an Airedale/sheepdog mix, became my first creature of habit. Her dietary and digestive needs regulated my days. Social and work schedules were adjusted accordingly.

When she was approaching 14 and could no longer navigate, my husband and I slept on the first floor and supported her on trips into the backyard. It took me awhile following her death to comprehend how much structure — and serenity — her presence imparted, how much it was needed and how much it was missed.

Five months later, we rescued Molly, an 8-year-old golden retriever, and six months later still, she rescued me when my husband suddenly died.

Molly needed to be fed, Molly needed to be walked, Molly needed care – and Molly needed me to perform these

Photo courtesy of Maryanne Malecki

Molly, a golden retriever, considered the "pond" in Maryanne's Malecki's Schenectady backyard to be a doggy day spa.

tasks. At least four times each day, I hurled my body out the front door, willed one foot in front of the other, and forced myself to reconnect with the world.

My upended existence had one grounding wire, one rudder, one creature of habit that could not be denied. It is not an overstatement to say that Molly preserved my life as I would come to know it.

My third creature of habit is Rufus, 5, who was born four days before Molly's death. A pony-sized designer mutt, the product of a golden retriever and standard poodle – aka goldendoodle — he somehow embodies both Molly and Tess in his appearance and temperament, plus a soupçon of enthusiasm all his own. A

total momma's boy, he fills the house with palpable energy.

Raising Rufus, particularly in those early days, eclipsed and assuaged episodes of grief, loneliness and sorrow, sadness and especially self-pity. Those don't last too long at puppy pre-K classes and puppy play dates.

When Rufus is at doggy day care, the house is strangely vacant. I'm once again free-ranging; my day is fluid, ungoverned — until I pick him up. Then order (of a sort) is restored, and all is right with our world. My time, his time, our time — each day, each week contains an allotment for each. Habit. Structure. Ritual. I wouldn't have it any other way.

▶ *Contributor Maryanne Malecki lives in Schenectady.*

German shepherds offered companionship

By Sue Nicholson

N ick, a fabulous German shepherd, was part of our life for 13 years during the 1970s. A natural charmer, he was the talk of Schenectady, where we operated a dog training school.

He did countless community events. He could count, jump through hoops and perform obedience to perfection. He was a distraction to the many dogs that took training lessons, chasing his ball while they were in class.

My husband, John, and I took him on our first date to the drive-in to see "King Kong." A guy was walking around dressed as King Kong and Nick befriended him.

He took his role in our lives very seriously and we enjoyed every minute we had him.

Time passed quickly and the gregarious puppy became an old gentleman. He stopped eating, had spondylosis and just couldn't go on. Our veterinarian came to our house and, after a dish of vanilla fudge ice cream, Nick went over the Rainbow Bridge where all best dogs go.

We later moved to Arizona where, in 2009, I saw this on Craigslist in the pet section: "Here are the dogs on the Rescue list. Time is running OUT!!!! Andy has until 5 PM Today to be Rescued!!!!!"

After work, John and I went to the Pima County Animal Shelter in Tucson. A volunteer

Photo courtesy of Sue Nicholson

This picture of Sue Nicholson's German shepherd, Nick, ran in the Times Union on May 6, 1979.

had been helpful when I called to say we would take him as soon as we could get there. She had Andy on a leash. We did the paperwork, paid the fees and took Andy home.

He was quiet, grateful and very, very old. He was wonderful with our three cats and our sheltie. He adapted to our routine and I felt like he had been ours forever.

We later rescued Oakley, a German shepherd, from the same shelter. Andy developed

glaucoma and went blind and Oakley became his leader.

Eventually, Andy developed significant medical problems. We knew it was time to make the decision to relieve him of his pain and discomfort. He left us to remember what a privilege it had been to share our life for a few years.

▶ *Contributor Sue Nicholson is from Schenectady and lives in Arizona.*

Happiness returns home when Kellie Anne arrives

Photos courtesy of Jennifer Patterson

Kellie Anne, a pit bull mix, enjoys a bone on her orthopedic dog bed.

By Jennifer Patterson

My heart sank as soon as I saw his number on caller ID.

It was a Monday afternoon about five years ago and my fiancé, Chris, had taken the day off to take his childhood dog to the vet with his mom. He was crying.

"Jennie had a tumor in her chest the size of a grapefruit," he said while trying to choke back tears. "That's why she was having trouble breathing."

A liver-and-white English springer spaniel with doe eyes and freckles, Jennie came home with Chris one day after he worked on a family friend's farm. He likes to say that he was paid in puppy.

It didn't take long for his parents to warm up to the mischievous runt, who greeted her humans with a Booda chew toy, squeals and piddles of excitement when they came home.

When Chris moved out of his parents' house and in with me, Jennie stayed behind. There was no disrupting their rhythm — morning toast dipped in coffee, pasta and meatballs in the afternoon and ice cream at night.

That's how things remained until a Sunday in December, just before the holidays. We knew something was wrong when Jennie — the dog whose butt wiggled whenever she was happy — couldn't lift her head to say goodbye.

When we went to Chris' parents' house for dinner the following Sunday, there was a heaviness in the air. No Jennie. No squeals. No wiggling butt. We even missed cleaning up the puddles.

By the next weekend, Chris' parents were woebegone. For years, they had Chris and his brother to take care of. When the boys were grown, there was Jennie to baby. Now that she was gone, there was not only a hole in their hearts, but also in their home.

By chance, I came across the picture of a dog up for adoption named Chiquita, like the banana, while skimming through my hometown paper. She sat just like Jennie used to — with one foot out like a rabbit — and gazed out at me with quizzical dark eyes and her head cocked to one side.

A few days later, Chris and

This newspaper cutout is the first photograph of Kellie Anne ever taken and still hangs on the refrigerator.

I took a ride with his parents to the Animal Shelter of Schoharie Valley in Howes Cave to see if she was still available.

The staff at the shelter was hesitant to let us meet the 9-month-old stray pegged as a pit bull mix. They were worried she was too big for Chris' mom, who walks with a cane. But we persisted, and they relented.

I was surprised by how timid she was when they brought her out from the kennels, tail between her legs. Judging from the marks on her backside, it looked like she had been shot with a BB gun.

Chris' dad was the first

to kneel down, and that dog wouldn't stop kissing his face. There were tears in his eyes when he stood up and asked, "Can we take her home today?"

The rest, as they say, is history. Kellie Anne, formerly known as Chiquita, got settled in what seemed like minutes and promptly became queen of her domain.

After much debate over her breed, we bought a dog DNA test kit. Kellie tips the scales at 100 pounds, so we weren't all that surprised by the results – a Rottweiler/Mastiff mix, or "full-figured lady," as Chris' dad likes to say.

Kellie has two favorite pastimes: giving kisses and getting kisses. When she isn't busy hiding treats and bones around the house, it's imperative that someone pets her at all times – paws will fly until she gets her way.

The similarities between her temperament and Jennie's are striking, but Kellie's almost human sensitivity, and her immeasurable capacity to love and be loved, is like no other dog I've come across.

Although we technically rescued her, it was Kellie's presence that healed the collective heart of Chris' family. For the first time in a long time, being there felt like coming home.

▶ *Contributor Jennifer Patterson lives in Guilderland and works at the Times Union.*

Good golly, Ms. Molly, cockapoo extraordinaire

By Sylvia-Jean Poggi

While reading the Times Union's classified ads one day, I came across an ad under "Dogs" of a litter of cockapoo puppies for sale. Not knowing much about this breed, I researched it and found that it was a crossbreed between a poodle and cocker spaniel.

Cockapoos are considered extremely loyal and loving, have great dispositions and are good with kids. It had been a few years since my miniature schnauzer, Little Chef, had passed on and in my grief, hadn't I vowed never again to own another dog like that remarkable little guy? I decided to go look at the puppies, but that was all. Just look.

I was hooked the minute I saw this 12-week-old black ball of fluff. I instantly fell in love with a tiny girl that had the bushiest tail, wagging fiercely like a dust mop, and weighed all of 3 pounds.

I named my new companion Ms. Molly and she had all the behaviors that I've come to love in a pet. I wish I could report that Ms. Molly did some special achievements, like those famous dogs Lassie or Rin Tin Tin did in the movies. But those things never happened. She was my loyal sweetheart in my home and life.

For 17 years, she watched over me. When I was happy, so was she, and she showed it as her little tail just thumped away. Without fail, she pa-

Photo courtesy of Sylvia-Jean Poggi

Ms. Molly is decorated with a festive bow for Christmas 1998.

trolled the inside of the house and backyard every single day. She carried her pink dolly through the house before we retired and slept with it in her little bed. Toward the end of her life, she still managed to do all her household rituals.

Though in pain, she never gave in to it. When her muzzle had become gray with age, her body grew frail with incurable illnesses and our nights were filled with sleeplessness, I knew it was time for us to say goodbye.

The last day with Ms. Molly brought sadness. We made that final visit to the veterinarian

and I kissed her goodbye.

It has been several years since that day, and I now have two other dogs: a Lhasa Apso named Lilyann and Princess Daisy, an Italian greyhound. These two give me just as much joy as Ms. Molly did. However, there would be no more promises against ever owning another dog. When you have committed yourself to loving a dog, and receive its absolute and unconditional love in return, it is hard to say you will never get another.

▶ *Contributor Sylvia-Jean Poggi lives in Schenectady.*

Sadie's love helps family through tragedy

By Lori Rodino

Photo courtesy Renee Bernard

Rachel Rodino, 7, sleeps with her golden retriever puppy, Sadie.

Our 6-year-old daughter, Rachel, was diagnosed with Huntington's disease in 2008 and I knew she didn't have much time left. Knowing my other children, Gianna and Anthony, were going to need something to love and hold on to with Rachel's passing, I told them if they could agree on a breed, we would get a dog.

My husband's great friend wanted to get them a puppy, and they never realized why I was doing this.

They decided on a golden retriever. My only request was that it be a female. I'm not sure why this gender, maybe I felt that she would nurture them through this difficult time.

We named her Sadie.

As a puppy, Sadie bit at the kids' toes. Her teething stage was difficult for the kids to understand but when I put the dog up on the hospital bed with Rachel, Sadie became a different puppy.

She would lie on Rachel's legs when she had a seizure and stay there until it passed. It was as if the puppy understood what to do. Every time I lifted Rachel off the hospital bed and put her on the couch to change the sheets, Sadie would lie on her legs before I could turn around and put a blanket on her.

As Rachel was failing, she and I visited hospice regularly and always came home after a few days. We had a routine: I pulled down the hospital bed at home and brought Rachel's things in and then got her out of the car.

Sadie became accustomed to this routine and couldn't wait to lie with Rachel.

I'll never forget the day Rachel passed. We had been in hospice for three days. When I came home without Rachel, trying to comfort Gianna and Anthony, there was Sadie staring at the hospital bed, waiting for her Rachel. The puppy wouldn't leave the bed. I had to call hospice to have them pick up the bed that day because Sadie was so sad and confused.

She's 6 years old, continues to take care of our family, always there when my husband falls and taking care of my Anthony and Gianna, sensing their anxiety or sadness.

You see, my husband and Gianna and Anthony all have Huntington's disease. There is no cure yet and Sadie knows her job is still to take care of our family. I will forever be grateful for Sadie. She gives us unconditional love, support and laughter every day. I don't know what we would do without her.

▶ *Contributor Lori Rodino lives in Guilderland.*

Lyla always knew the right thing to do

By Valerie Tabak

As one of 13 puppies, Lyla, our loyal chocolate Labrador, became our chosen one at the age of 6 weeks when she and her five sisters were brought to our house for the meet-and-greet.

We felt our 11-year-old son, who was diagnosed with Asperger's syndrome, would benefit from the life lessons dog ownership can provide. Who better to teach about loyalty and trust than a dog?

We registered for "puppy preschool" and our son assumed the role of alpha dog. He was more than willing to learn everything that he could about training a puppy, read voraciously on the topic and practiced what we learned.

Sometimes, he practiced methods that he decided were better than the instructor's, sometimes he told the instructor about his methods and always Lyla's response was loyalty, obedience and enthusiasm.

When he was lonely, he could talk to Lyla, snuggle up to her and share what was known to only them. When my son needed to burn off some energy, Lyla eagerly followed.

The years flew, Lyla grew into a beautiful adult dog and was adored by all.

In the spring of 2002, I was diagnosed with stage 3 inflammatory breast cancer

Photo courtesy of Valerie Tabak

Valerie Tabak with Lyla near a lake, a favorite spot for a water dog.

and started a journey that kept me away from work for a year. It was then that I learned the comfort and companionship that Lyla could afford to me. As I lay in bed, Lyla would appear next to me, position her body close to me and effect a posture of guardianship and nurturing. She was never invited on to the bed, she had never been a dog to jump on to the bed, but nonetheless, there she was when she was needed.

Frequently, I asked myself, "How can a dog know what to do when so many humans are incapable of expressing their feelings and emotions?"

The summer of 2010, diving off the dock, following us swimming in the Great Sacandaga, around and around the boat on the mooring ball, she gasped while her COPD

made her audible breathing difficult for me to bear.

Up the ladder, proudly standing at the bow of the boat, wind blowing her ears, these were Lyla's happy moments.

The day we drove her to the veterinary hospital to provide her with the dignified ending of which she was so deserving, my husband and I said nothing to one another.

Our son sat in the back seat with her and whispered words known only to them. As we walked her into the building, she followed my son. We stayed with her as she closed her eyes and we thanked her for being the best dog ever.

▶ *Contributor Valerie Tabak lives in Guilderland.*

Older dog plays teacher to young dog

By Dan Chouiniere

My wife and I spend a lot of time with our dogs, Morgan and Finn. They have unique personalities and have become such a part of our lives.

Finn, our 18-month-old yellow Lab, sleeps as hard as he plays, and waking him for any reason takes a bit of effort. Quite often in the evening, after a great play session and walk, Finn will jump up into our recliner, hang his head off the side armrest and snore — so loudly that we have to turn up the TV just to hear. His best snore session happened one night when he brought his ball inside the house. He loves that thing so much that he decided to sleep with it in his mouth, only making the snoring louder.

Morgan has learned to accept Finn since we brought him into our house last year, although the younger dog annoys her due mainly to their age difference.

We'd like Finn to be an Air Scent search dog, if we can get him through basic good behavior. As we train Finn, Morgan always shows him that she can accomplish any command quickly. She looks at him with disgust that he doesn't know what to do. She does her best to show him what to do. I'm certain that after a few years, she will have taught him well.

Morgan loves fishing.

Photo courtesy of Dan Chouiniere

Morgan loves fishing.

She's not a dog who focuses really well — she is easily distracted by walkers, joggers or (heaven forbid) another dog crossing in front of our yard, turning into the most vicious guard dog ever, or at least she thinks so. If a squirrel, chipmunk or other rodent wanders into the yard, she will immediately stop what she is doing and make sure they leave or face her wrath.

All distraction disappears when the fishing gear appears, especially when it is accompanied by my fishing kayak.

She loves fishing so much that I had to buy a fishing kayak so she didn't have to wait on shore when I fished out in the lake. A platform behind me is designed for fishing gear, but I've rigged it for my dog's comfort so she can fish with me from the kayak as well as from shore.

She's as happy as can be floating along, waiting patiently for a tug on the fishing line to see if I'll catch anything. She's quite content spending time with me on the lake.

We walk the dogs twice a day and spend as much quality time with them as we can. All of the time we are with them enriches our lives as much as theirs.

▶ *Contributor Dan Chouiniere lives in Halfmoon.*

BB loved snowstorms

By Ross N. Gleason

Photo courtesy of Ross N. Gleason

BB, Baby Bear, a Pekingese.

When I got married and had kids, I resisted the idea of getting a dog. My reasons were perfectly practical — the commitment, the expense, pet sitting ...

When we were living in Virginia, I came home from a military Reserves weekend one Sunday afternoon and my youngest daughter, Christine, thrust this white fluff ball into my arms. I scowled but knew I had lost the battle. In truth, I was glad.

The little fluff ball was BB, Baby Bear, a Pekingese. The next 17 years were quite something.

Although he was a purebred, BB had a cataract in one eye, which made him a "family dog" and our good fortune.

He was intelligent, stubborn with a capital "S," fearless, feisty, funny, crazy and unfailingly loyal to Christine. He was a gourmet and liked eating his dog food from a plate on the table and sipping his champagne.

In Vermont, he patrolled the inside perimeter of our fenced-in yard. He was the alpha dog and brought up a golden retriever, German shepherd and two Pekingese rescue puppies, Fizzgig and Maggie.

Winter was his time of year. The first snowstorm we had, I took him out and tossed him in a snow drift. He worked his way out, covered with snow, and never looked back. He went sledding with the girls,

sitting right up front. He made trails in the snow and hiked the trails and cleaned his face by sticking it in the snow. He loved to take snow baths.

BB chose the house we live in. He made a complete circuit of the yard, came back, plopped himself down and wouldn't move.

At Christmas, he would plop himself under the tree, with gifts under it, and nap. Sometimes, he was hard to find. His favorite place on Christmas morning was in the center of things, usually under a pile of wrapping paper.

It seems you don't really understand what a pet means to you or what a saga it has been until his health starts to fail or he's gone. My family had BB for 17 years. Every time we looked around he was there.

He made four long-distance moves with us. The kids grew up with him.

BB didn't really show much sign of aging until his 16th year. He spent more and more time sleeping in his favorite spot next to the hearth behind the rocking chair. It became more difficult to rouse him.

He was stubborn until the end. When the time came, he went to sleep in his favorite spot by the hearth. When my wife came home from work this time, he wouldn't wake up.

We still miss him after nine years. I don't admit it to my wife, but I still look for him once in a while when I'm not thinking.

▶ *Contributor Ross N. Gleason, formerly of Colonie, lives in Vestal, Broome County.*

No more throws for Ivory

Ivory catches a Frisbee thrown by owner Paul Grondahl in 1995. Fetching a Frisbee was one of the favorite activities for the yellow Labrador retriever mix. She had to be put down in 1995 while still in her prime at age 9 due to complications of cancer.

By Paul Grondahl

Driving west on I-88, bound for Ithaca, heading straight into a sunset so bright not even sunglasses could shield its intensity, Ivory lay dying in the back seat, curled up on her favorite blue blanket, nearly motionless, a placid comma of yellow fur where just four days earlier there had been an ecstatic exclamation point. Reaching back to stroke the dog's listless body, from the driver's seat I could touch only her left hind paw. So I caressed that and rubbed its fearful, spiritless pads. She suddenly seemed small, this once powerful, fiercely athletic animal that had lived up to her Labrador retriever breeding and chased sticks, balls, Frisbees — anything that could be thrown across grassy meadows, over snowy fields, through streams and ponds. For nine years, since she was just 6 weeks old and could nestle in two cupped hands, she had been a faithful companion.

Heading toward the Cornell

University College of Veterinary Medicine, I talked to her, recounting the adventures over the years, the camping trips and hikes, other travels.

"We see a lot of cancer in dogs this age," the local veterinarian had said. There wasn't much my vet could do, or say. The blood work showed Ivory's liver and kidneys had given out. She was dying slowly from the inside, although she was four or five years shy of her life expectancy.

On the previous Friday, she was running and leaping to catch a Frisbee. On Saturday, she threw up. On Sunday, she was weak from not touching food or water in two days. On that Monday, she could barely stand when I brought her to the vet. On Tuesday, she made it through the night. The intravenous drip only made her throw up again. As it was, she probably wouldn't live to see Wednesday. My vet was helpful and made the arrangements at Cornell.

I left work late that afternoon and drove 200 miles. It seemed Ivory deserved that much. She had given unconditional love since I picked her out of an abandoned litter up for adoption at an animal shelter.

In 35 years, I have had other dogs and cats, but Ivory became my shadow like no other pet. She was my dog and existed solely to please me. She awoke with my first stirrings each morning without fail, trembling with anticipation, a tennis ball stuffed in her mouth, tail beating out a rhythm of giddiness on the door and walls with the certainty of a metronome. "Ivory, your tail is not a baseball bat," my 5-year-old son, Sam, would say after her tail-wagging cleared a shelf of his toy trucks or gave the groggy boy a resounding wake-up whack in the chest.

And when I dressed each morning for work, there was Ivory, sitting at my feet in ritual silence, entreating me with a hang-dog look. I'd get my shirt and pants on and, still in socks, more often than not I'd give in to her silent pleading. "'Come on," I'd say, and up she'd jump, my hands clutching her front paws to my chest, her long body stretched to its full length, the dog looking me nearly square in the eyes. And we'd dance. The ridiculous scene always made Sam laugh. Waltzing with Ivory. We never tangoed. I had my limits. Sometimes, though, I'd sing in a high-pitched yowl that made Ivory bark crazily as we shuffled across the rug. This would get Sam laughing so hard he'd almost cry.

For nine years, Ivory was central to the daily rhythm of the day. The morning walk, the evening romp and Frisbee toss, the late-night walk just before bed. And then the tail-thumping wake-up call started the cycle all over again.

Home, it seems, is where the dog is.

At Cornell, the vet said he couldn't operate until morning, and she might not make it. Surgery was a shot in the dark, and costly. Even if she survived, Ivory would need to spend a week or more in the intensive care unit and the chances of her returning to her former Frisbee-catching vigor were not good. The only certainty left to me was to choose an injection that would put her to sleep. The vet simply explains the options. He does not help you make the choice.

I agonized for four hours at the hospital as Ivory lay dying, wondering what was best, gauging my need to hold onto this companion versus the dog's desire to be released from her pain. Then, I held her slack head, looked into her distant, sickly eyes and spoke to her through a stream of tears as the drug did its work and she breathed her last.

"So Ivory just went to sleep and will never wake up, Dad?" That's right, I assured Sam. My son likes to remember her curio-clearing tail and the waltzing. I will always think of Ivory catching the Frisbee, her favorite activity. I could heave the disc until my arm was sore, but she would always run back with it, drop the Frisbee at my feet and bark for one more throw. Even when dusk had cloaked us and it became difficult to see, she'd bark for one more throw. Just one more. I can picture Ivory now racing off into the gathering darkness, her coiled energy springing upward for the Frisbee. There is a sublime moment that follows the leap when all four paws have left the ground, and for a split second, she is no longer of the Earth, soaring into the shadows.

▶ *This article first appeared in the Times Union in June 1995.*

Hamlet – A celebration of the running life

By Vince Juliano

Photo courtesy of Vince Juliano

Hamlet, a chocolate Lab, loved to run and hike with his owners.

He was supposed to be her dog.

My wife, Emily, grew up in rural Cazenovia, where she and her sister Amanda trained Labradors as aide dogs and welcomed strays, along with a variety of other pets. Emily loved all animals no matter how seemingly insignificant.

After our marriage in 2000, we discussed getting a pet. I read a New York Times article about a dog everyone loved in Central Park. His name was Hamlet. I liked the name.

That Christmas, Emily and I visited a breeder and chose a male chocolate Lab pup. We named him Hamlet.

One by one, the rules I set disappeared. The second night of whining in the crate led to Hamlet sleeping in our bed. Hamlet loved his creature comforts, he loved food, but most of all he loved us. Despite his pedigree, he showed no interest in hunting or chasing wildlife. Other dogs piqued his interest briefly, but after initial greetings, he moved on.

Hamlet was very intelligent with traits more human than canine. He was cautious, sensitive, non-alpha and loved human companionship.

We were avid runners and also loved to cross-country ski. Hamlet was quickly introduced to our active lifestyle and adapted well. He was passionate about being included and did not want to stay home.

The Jonestown 10-miler is a grand prix running event in New England. Emily was developing into one of the top distance runners in the region and 4-month-old Hamlet joined us for the first of his many road trips to competitive running events. At the awards ceremony, Emily had to share the attention with young Hamlet, who earned his nickname that day — "Ham."

In the Salmon Hills of the Tug Hill plateau, Hamlet quickly learned how to follow behind my skis and in front of Emily in single file on snow-packed roads.

At Cape Breton, Nova Scotia, Emily, Hamlet and I ran a 7-mile round trip "rave run" several times each summer.

During Hamlet's dozen years, he traveled with us extensively, made many friends within the running community, walked, ran and slept in some of the most beautiful places on Earth.

I recently retired and purchased a log cabin home with acres of wooded land and a freshwater stream behind. Hamlet walked these wooded trails daily during his final six months. He never got old, and was running and hiking in his final weeks of life. His coat was still rich, his joints remained sound, as did his vision, hearing and appetite.

He was supposed to be Emily's dog and, of course, he was. He also became my best friend, in a celebration of life.

▶ *Contributor Vince Juliano lives in Delanson.*

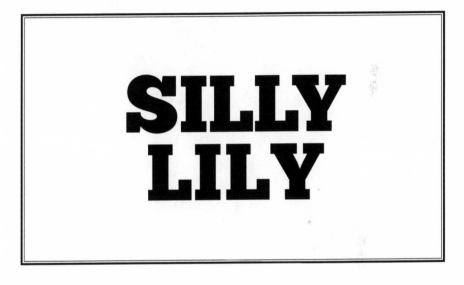

Reclaiming a dog's love

By Paul Grondahl

I placed Daisy's collar on the windowsill above the sink, along with a photo I took on her final day. The house was strangely quiet. There was no click-click, click-click of a dog's toenails on the hardwood floors, no more metallic tinkle of the rabies and name tags rubbing together whenever she moved. Her canine wind chime, as I had come to think of it, had fallen silent.

We grieved the loss of Daisy, each in our own way. Life went on. Caroline turned 18, summer ended and we dropped her off at college for her freshman year. We were empty-nesters, my wife Mary and I, and we learned how still a house can be.

Owning a dog is a matter of the heart, but now I was thinking with my head and considering the costs in a practical way. It is easy to become self-centered without a dog. We slept later. Long walks around the neighborhood ceased because they didn't make sense without a dog or a kid at home. I started feeling isolated and out of touch without the bonhomie of other dog people. I missed the easy sociability that comes with stopping to chat with neighbors I got to know because of our dogs.

Pragmatism cannot calculate the return on investment of a dog. A dog feeds the soul in incalculable ways. Dogs bring out our better selves. We were dog-deprived, and our family

Lori Van Buren / Times Union
Lily sits near the Moses statue in Washington Park in Albany.

was the poorer for it.

Our daughter Caroline — who took the loss of Daisy perhaps the hardest because the puppy was presented to her as a 4th birthday present — broke the ice after a year and began emailing me pictures of dogs for adoption. Ours was a silent conspiracy. We did not immediately loop in my wife, who seemed to be doing better than the two of us without a dog in the house. Caroline and I eventually fell hard for a photo of Lillian, a 2-year-old female Lab and pit bull mix for adoption through Out of the Pits, a not-for-profit group that champions American Pit Bull Terriers, a breed that has gotten a bad rap. Lillian was jet black, with a heart-shaped white patch on her chest and a back paw with a fleck of white on two toes. She reminded us a little bit of Daisy. We arranged

for a meeting with the young couple who owned her. They were moving and couldn't take Lillian with them.

Our hearts melted when we met her for the first time. She burrowed into Caroline's lap as we sat on our deck and got introduced to Miss Lillian, or Lily for short. The couple got her from the Adirondack Pitbull Rescue. The couple had taken good care of her and brought along immunization and veterinarian records. After five minutes, we said yes to Lily. She came to live with us the next day. Caroline and I went to the pet store and loaded up on gear with the giddiness of first-graders picking out new school supplies.

Almost immediately, the trouble began. Lily ricocheted around the house like a cyclone. She shuddered with anxiety and had accidents.

We left her alone for a short while and returned to find garbage strewn around the kitchen after she ripped the garbage bag out of a pull-out cabinet bin that she managed to yank open. She was like a toddler prone to tantrums if we left her side.

We retrieved the crate we used when Daisy was young. Lily broke out by bending heavy wire slats and climbing out the top. We reinforced the crate and called for assistance from our friend and neighbor, Gary Riviello, a retired state employee who started a pet care business. Gary walked Lily each day at lunchtime when Caroline was away at school and Mary and I were at work. Lily's anxiety eased. She started snuggling and became a 60-pound lap dog. It was nice to be speaking that strange hybrid language again, a sing-song baby talk where Ls become Ws and it sounds like a bad Barbara Walters imitation. We are not alone in the language of dogs. There is something sublime about scrunching up Lily's face and rubbing her velvety ears first thing in the morning and speaking doggy talk. You forget about early wake-ups, the extra work and expense. Researchers in Japan reported in a recent study that when dog owners gazed into their pets' eyes, oxytocin levels rose in the humans and the dogs, too, and a deep bond was formed.

Finally, science found a biological answer for the mysteries and astonishing depths of

Lily gives Mary Grondahl an early-morning greeting.

the human-canine bond.

Caroline was the first to let Lily sleep on her bed, and soon Mary and I caved, too. Caroline requests a daily photo or video of Lily when she's at college, and Mary usually obliges. I've taken Lily on a road trip to see Caroline at school in Manhattan and we spent the afternoon in Central Park, where we found a dog-friendly café that seated Lily and brought her a biscuit and water bowl.

That doesn't mean Lily has been cured of all her bad habits. Caroline started a list on the refrigerator of Lily casualties. She crunched Christmas tree light bulbs and chewed a disposable razor she fished out of a bathroom garbage can. She tore through, literally, the heavy spine of a hardcover Harry Potter book and an American Usage Dictionary. A slab of chocolate cake disappeared from a paper plate in the middle of the island in the kitchen, its foil covering untouched. That's why when we go from room to room, the sound of doors clacking shut

echoes down hallways. We've had to child-proof the place for our stealth toddler.

Lily has brought us moments I would not trade for anything, starting with wake-up calls of cuddles and kisses and full-body welcome wiggles when we come in the door after a few minutes or a few hours outside. She rests her head on our shoulders like a young child and loves to spoon if given the chance. I love to see Lily as she rests her paws on Caroline's hips and the two of them waltz around the kitchen. Mary talks in a sing-song voice as she points her iPad and narrates a video she'll email to Caroline. Lily races up the stairs and waits on the top landing to make sure we're still behind her, before she leaps onto the bed in a blur of comforter-clearing exuberance — followed by curling up on the pillows like a semicolon denoting a brief pause.

Lily is the fastest, most athletic dog we've ever had and I like to take her on rides as she runs alongside my mountain bike. I never had a dog with whom I felt comfortable enough to try this. Her strides match each revolution of my pedals, her ears pinned back by the wind and her gaze fixed in a Zen-like stare.

We are moving as one, poetry in motion, and I wonder how or why we ever lived without a dog.

▶ *pgrondahl@timesunion. com* ▪ *518-454-5623* ▪ *@ PaulGrondahl*

Index of contributors

Credits

PROJECT EDITORS

Teresa Buckley

Paul Grondahl

ART DIRECTOR

Carin Lane

COPY EDITORS

Tim Blydenburgh

Keshia Clukey

Susan Mehalick

Joe Stalvey

Lisa Morey Stevens

SYSTEM SUPPORT

Jim White

ONLINE PRODUCERS

Paul Block

Trudi Shaffer

ON THE WEB

To see more stories and photos,
watch videos and purchase
additional copies of this book:
http://timesunion.com/greatdogs